Through The Eyes of A Daughter

Felicia S.

Queen Dream Publishing

Through The Eyes of A Daughter, Fathers We Need
Copyright © 2012 by Felicia Smith
Edited by: Zach Martin
Illustrator: Joyce Fler Reyes

All rights reserved. No part of this book may be reproduced or transmitted in any form or by any means without written permission from the author.

ISBN (978-0985143312)
Library of Congress Control: 2012902755

"Scriptures taken from the HOLY BIBLE, NEW INTERNATIONAL VERSION®. Copyright © 1973, 1978, 1984 by International Bible Society. Used by permission of Zondervan Publishing House. All rights reserved."

Printed in USA by 48HrBooks (www.48HrBooks.com)

Disclaimer:
Although the Author and Publisher have made every effort to ensure the accuracy & completeness of information presented in this book, we assume no responsibility for errors, inaccuracies, omissions or any inconsistency herein. Any slights of people, places or organizations are unintentional.

Author's Autograph Page

To:

From:

Dedication for you and Special Thanks for Others

From my heart to yours, I dedicate this book to those who saw what I saw, felt what I felt, cried like I cried, and felt disappointment as I have. In essence, I dedicate this to you, reader. If, in some form or fashion, you had not been through the same things as me, my guess is you'd be reading something else.

My hope is that you'll learn, heal, hope, but most importantly forgive if that's what you need to do. There are, however, are a few treasured people I wish to acknowledge & thank and surely they know who they are. These people stood with me as this came to life, as I gave birth to this book and published it so thank you. Heavenly Father: there isn't enough room to continue thanking you because, as much as you've done, I could never repay you. Thank you for the unconditional love no one can replace. Thank you God, the Father of all fathers!

Table of Contents

Dedication and Special Thanks…………………………….4
Introduction for Fathers: Your Children ………………….8
Chapter 1: My Story: What I Learned……………………13
Chapter 2: My Father's Stories…………………………...23
Chapter 3: Fatherless Statistics…………………………..60
Chapter 4: For Daughters: Is It Abuse?…………………..69
Chapter 5: Dad with "Overwhelmed"……………………89
Chapter 6: Dad with "Homeless and Searching"………..119
Chapter 7: "I Apologize"…………....…………………..155
Chapter 8: Homeless to Found..…………………..…….158
Chapter 9: Seen Through These Eyes…………………..161
Chapter 10: A Daughter's Prayer………………………...164
Meet the Author……………………………………….167

Introduction for Fathers
No Matter What, Provide for Your Children
"If anyone does not provide for his immediate family, he has denied the faith and is worse than an unbeliever."
—*1 Timothy 5:8*

The question I'm asking is, Isn't she lovely, isn't she wonderful? Does anything make you feel better than the first time you see your little bundle of preciousness swaddled in that pink blanket? That's *your* precious little girl. That caption on the bassinet that reads "It's a Girl"? That's your daughter they're talking about.

Fast forward. You see, fathers have a profound effect on what a daughter does, how she acts, what she thinks, and ultimately who she becomes. It all depends on the relationship you two share. The choice is as simple as deciding whether you'd have her be blessed or cursed. Whether you're a new father or a seasoned one, take a look at your little pumpkin's face. She needs you. Remember that Steve Wonder song: *Isn't she lovely?* To you, she really should be.

When you think your little girl isn't looking, think again. Little do you know that your love, your deeds, and especially your words have a profound effect on this precious vessel God has entrusted to you as a father. Know this: she is looking, she is watching, she is feeding off your love, affection, and protection. When you're denying her those things, you're starving her. Which will you do, fathers, prevail or fail? My hope is that you'll prevail.

Realize that you are the head and not the tail. You'd benefit from seeking God if you don't know how to be a father. That being the case, you may need to get with good fathers who can provide wisdom and understanding on how to be a good father or even one who is proud to be called daddy. Surround yourself with great role models that can help propel you to becoming the father you need to be. After all, wouldn't you like to be the daddy to daddy's little girl?

Believe it or not, this book is credited to both of my fathers. On the one hand, God the father gave me the vision to write this volume, but my paternal father gave me the urgency—out of hurt, frustration and pain—to go forward with it. I was finally living closer to my father, the earthly steward who gave me life and who hadn't lived in the same state as me for sixteen years, when it happened again: rejection, frustration, and all the characteristics of that toxic relationship between daughters and fathers.

Living in close quarters revealed to me the true relationship that truly had never existed between me and my father. It was the same rejection I had felt from a man or two of interest in my life, so the feeling of rejection was familiar. I report these feelings of rejection from dad and from male love interests sadly, for I knew they were unhealthy and something not of God. As often as I could to relieve the heartache, I'd run away from similar relationships. Even the slightest resemblances to these unhealthy relationships when I became an adult were often too much to bear. In the end I always ran.

After running so much from love as adult I realized that running was not the answer. At that point I began seeking my real father, God. This father, the Alpha & Omega, provided something no one else was capable of providing. He showed me that, just as I am a daughter of two, I am made for a mate (*Genesis 2:18*) so in running away from relationships I was running away from God.

All this to say, no one is perfect; in fact, man is designed to disappoint. Ultimately, our supreme trust is in God only (*Proverbs 3:4-5*). Fathers, the impact you have all depends on the difference you make in the lives of those around you, especially the lives of your daughters. The question I pose is: Fathers, how much will your weaknesses affect your daughters' lives? The choice is up to you. Read this book and discover just how profound the disappointment can be for those who share their lives with you. As a father, ask yourself: How will my household be affected by my love, my input, and my support, or the lack thereof?

Know that you need to spend quality time with your kids to nurture them, to nurture the desires and dreams that will lead them to discover their calling in life. Fathers, your sound direction is vital to your children. When they share their dreams for the future, take a moment to listen. When they lose their way, help guide them back to safe ground. If you dismiss, disregard, and blatantly belittle their dreams, you're dismissing, disregarding, and belittling them as a person. Take the time to plan their future together.

Chapter 1
My Story: What I Learned

Fathers, how do you evaluate yourself as a dad? I don't think you realize that little girls grow up to be ladies looking not only for love and acceptance from dad, but also from their respective mates. We look to be celebrated, honored, adored, and truly loved for the good in us and, yes, the bad too, since we are imperfect beings. When daddy's little girl can't get this type of love and attention that celebrates and affirms her at home, guess what? She tries to find it in other places. And then you wonder why she's a teenage mother. I'd encourage you to not neglect your daughters, take the focus off of only yourselves, and spend time really seeking a healthy relationship with your little girls. It's not that all fathers fit this description, but I speak to you as someone who had a front row seat to a corrosive father-daughter relationship. Dad did spend some time with me, but it wasn't often and it wasn't quality time.

If other women have your focus instead of your own daughter, you're not putting your wife and your daughter(s) first in your life. If you're not putting your wife or your daughter(s) first, who are you putting before them? Carefully consider the impact of your answer.

Ponder on the question, what kind of legacy are you leaving for your children? Do you leave a legacy of peace or problems? If you want to know which it should be, read *Proverbs 13:22*. Let your legacy be something worth remembering. Or haven't you given any thought to something so important? What will your obituary read? How will you be remembered in your eulogy? What words will your loved ones choose to remember you by? More importantly, what will your children say about you when you're gone? What do they say about you *now*? If you really care, you'll pursue righteous answers to these questions.

Don't leave generational curses. Rather, work to leave generational blessings for your children. Look at it like this: you can force your children's generation to start over by rebuilding from hurt memories, or you can start them off right, with fun, loving, supportive memories. Imagine where they might be able to go building off that kind of firm foundation. You have more than the ability to do what no other man can do for your family: be a father to those children who need you! Trust me, this is the truth.

You have to admit, if you're telling yourself the truth that you would be ashamed for your kids not to even care about attending your funeral. My prayer is you'll realize that you want to be missed when you're gone and that you'll work toward a healthier legacy, instead of one that shames you or your family provided this is your case. This is my sound prayer for you.

Men, since you are the head and not the tail, would you like your children re-living the same issues you've encountered? Give your children examples they can live by. Let them adopt your good habits rather than those that are unhealthy, abusive, or lacking in faith.

Our society offers them many unhealthy role models so seeing your healthy role model is ideal. Allow them the chance to see life, not limitations. Your attitude towards them determines their altitude in life. What would you have for your children's heritage: a good model leading them to a healthy life in spirit or filled with darkness? We all know the world already offers unlimited models of darkness.

I am so grateful for my heavenly father. With God and his Word I've discovered a newfound confidence, an interdependence that doesn't leave me relying on others who might disappoint me because of their own problems. Before fully understanding the role God could play in my life, I sought approval everywhere, only to experience countless episodes of rejection. What I realized is that, because I never felt full acceptance from my father, I wanted and needed it desperately from other men. This opened the doors to a world of unhealthy living and, fathers; you definitely don't want this for your little girls. Even if your little girl is at this point is a grown woman, and unless she's already married to a great son-in-law, you have time to help her by loving her, by supporting her, and by showing her what men are capable of accomplishing through their love. If you are still married to her mother, your daughter sees how you treat her mom. If you treat your daughter's mother well, your daughter will seek out that same strength, love, and support in her future relationships, including marriage.

Growing up, my idea of a father was someone who guided the strength of the family, the rock, the person you know will be there no matter what. A father was the one who would be at a daughter's birth, watch her first baby steps, come to her dance recitals, and be waiting at home before the high school prom, waiting to frighten the guy taking his little girl on her first date. My idea of a father was someone who would be there on every step of the path from girlhood to womanhood. That's what a father is. We women need our dads for all the important moments of our lives as we grow into womanhood.

The Bible speaks about celebrating and honoring your father (*Ephesians 6:2*). If you are a dad, can you picture yourself being honored and celebrated? What I know, felt, and saw as a little girl was a silhouette of a man who was there in body but emotionally absent. I never felt that strong connection with my father. Growing up, my dad didn't know either of his dads, heavenly or paternal, so this is a relatable matter. I ask myself, is this one of the reasons we felt he never truly connected with his children or is it that he did not want to ever be a dad? I tend to think becoming an unprepared father is not worth the hurt or hindrance it causes to the innocent child. At this point, if you are a father-to-be, prepare yourself ahead of time by following God the father, who loves his children, as an example.

As a child I struggled with never being able to call my father "Daddy." For me, this was a huge setback early in life. I especially think this was an emotional disconnection for me. My dad told me as a child not to call him "Dad," but rather to acknowledge him by calling him by his first name. This was too much for a little girl to interpret. When you're not able to call your dad "Daddy," it triggers a feeling of not being accepted by the one who made you. Remember, words have power, so anything you say to your daughter, especially if it isn't supportive, can plant the wrong seeds. Calling your daddy by his first name makes you feel like you are not his child at all. It makes you feel fatherless because you want to call him daddy and be accepted, loved, and supported by all means. Fathers, I imagine allowing your daughters to call you "Daddy" makes your little girl feel like a princess.

Fathers, you rob your little girl that privilege when you don't connect with her early in life. For those of you who need to work on building this father-daughter connection, I encourage you to make the effort. For the rest of you, I salute you in advance for making a conscious effort to head off these problems before they ever occur.

Your children need to connect with you, dad. They need your love and your acceptance. More importantly, they need you! Don't forget you were chosen and given the privilege as a man to bond with them and have also been given the honor of fatherhood. Don't be fooled at their ages if they have become adults. Your daughters still want to call you "Daddy" until either of you leaves this earth.

Many days when my father came home, he was argumentative, especially with my mom. It was not uncommon for me to be a witness to broken furniture and loud yelling, followed by uncomfortable silence. As I think back, I remember our household being one that had more memories you'd want to forget than remember. As a family unit, I remember pain, loss, and struggle.

If you are willing to allow your family's legacy to mirror this story, there's nothing you need to do. But, if you care to leave behind your love, good times, and supportive attention to your children, then by all means take the time to be a father. Please be that daddy that your little girl and your family as a whole needs. You have been appointed and handpicked by God for this task.

In my childhood home, through my two eyes, I saw two people entrusted to be role models for four children. Unfortunately, the nature of my parents' relationship, served as a negative example. There were many days that my parents fought as a result of one of them verbally provoking the other. The power of words is simple, but profound (*James 1:3*).

I can tell you that life, a lot of it, was terrible for our family while I was growing up. I wish I had more positive memories that I could take away from my childhood experience, but it seems I was the daughter of a man ill-prepared to serve as a father figure.

When divorce split up our family, the quiet environment we experienced as a result of no fussing and fighting sounded very much like peace, the peace we needed after so many harsh rounds of bitter words. It was just what the doctor ordered. We were all left broken after the divorce and needed healing in our own ways. Do you, fathers, really want to be remembered as a bitter voice in your home? I think not. Examine yourself, have a talk with yourself in the mirror. If you want, consult the man in the mirror.

Sure, it is more common these days for many couples to be unmarried and have children. Those divided households should have no detrimental effect on you being there for your children.

Guys, even if the mother makes life difficult for you, be there for your children. I am aware some situations are awful between unmarried parents and that being absent is more peaceful than being present, but remember your children. In the short term, your absence is more convenient, but the long term effect can prove damaging. Overall, more than seventy-five percent of American children are at risk because of paternal deprivation. Even in two-parent homes, fewer than twenty-five percent of young boys and girls experience an average of at least one hour a day of individual contact with their fathers (Source: Henry Biller, "The Father Factor").

The only two that seem to win in this situation are you and your children's mother, but what about the children waiting to see their daddy? I can't express to you how much your daughter needs you, even if the time spent with your little princess is not as much as you both desire.

Make a resolution to be present and active in your daughter's life no matter what. Those quiet and convenient moments you choose to avoid her mother don't afford your little girl the option to have someone to take your respected place. Surely your mind can imagine what she might fill that place in her heart with: it might be an older man your daughter admires that spends time with her long enough to entice her into the back seat of his car, resulting in an unwanted pregnancy.

What about engaging in dangerous drugs and alcohol? Let's not forget the lifetime sexual diseases that too often exist, or going to a juvenile detention center or, worse, prison. 85% of all youths sitting in prisons grew up in a fatherless home (source: Fulton Co. Georgia jail populations, Texas Dept. of Corrections 1992). Is this something you want to trade for your peace and convenience? Regardless of the situation with your daughter's mother, be there for your daughter in your absence. Otherwise, someone else will be.

Legal options exist for you to be a part of your children's lives regardless of the relationship, or the lack thereof, with the mother. Don't let this type of distance with one person disturb your love, your time, your influential presence, and the fact that your kids need you, daddy.

Once your children are in this world and you have become a father, you simply have no choice but to fill the role. My dad elected to become a father it seems casually, just as many men do when they choose unprotected sex with their spouse, girlfriend, baby-mama-to-be, one-night-stands, or even prostitute. You make the choice to father each time you engage in sex, so you need to proactively prepare yourself or abstain from sex. Abstaining until you're married will eliminate the drama you'll encounter by becoming an unprepared father.

I'm only here, in love, to speak truth and intend to not judge, just offer real life experience. I realize men have many struggles to overcome, many forces and entities against them that tear them down. I only offer you the other side, that innocent being that receives what you as the father convey to your daughter. There are many children who may never tell you what they need, either because they are afraid or because they don't know to ask. You may not have a daughter who will let you know, but God knows. He knows it all. He knows your side and especially the other side, that daughter who longs just for you to be her daddy.

Chapter 2
My Father's Stories
"I am a walking Bible"
—My father

Chato, my father, was born in a non-Christian home where Catholicism was practiced. He became to know Christ or his Heavenly Father, God, until becoming an adult. He credits his second wife, who was a kind and devout Christian woman, with helping him find Christ.

Born in the 1950's in Colon, Panama, he came home from the hospital to a room that housed his six other siblings, his mother, his grandmother, and a great-grandmother. He says, "When my mother left for America to provide a better life for us back in Central America, she left behind many responsibilities for her kids, but even more responsibilities for our caretakers, my great uncles and great aunts. For the most part, me and my siblings were forced to make our own life decisions." I have to wonder, since I never asked, if my dad ever wanted to be a father. I have to admit when a man is excited to have kids you see preparation. You can see the happiness in the man.

Chato, whose nickname is "Shorty," attended Bolivia Public School. Between the ages of seven and twelve, he attended a Seventh Day Adventist school and was known for being the messenger for his grandmother and mother. Because of living conditions and a lack of support, Chato didn't complete high school. He later completed a certification program in auto body repair at a local community college. This proved to be beneficial later; he owned a lucrative detailing and auto body repair business for years in the Southwest.

"The separation of my mother and her children left room for many problems," Chato says. A generational seed was planted for her children to fend for themselves and that carried on into *their* children's generation as well. The grandfather I never knew was from Costa Rica and was known to be a medical doctor. From my dad's recollection, he only saw him once in his life, at the age of ten. Here's that resounding question: could this have been the reason for my dad being so disconnected from his own children? I don't think he ever learned how to connect, and surely that was one of the reasons. Could this be the case with many fatherless fathers? I would presume so.

Even during the few moments Chato visited with his dad, there wasn't a connection. In retrospect, their visits were built on the memory of pure rejection and a strong disconnect. Could this be the reason that pain roams inside the rejected child's heart? You see rejected little boys grow up to be rejected men acting out their pain in various ways. As it stands, he resents the fact that his mother, in his words, had an "adulterous lifestyle with married professional men." He describes her beauty as being the sole reason for such the behavior. Chato says that he does not want this behavior to repeat itself again, even yes in me, his only daughter, since he too is aware of generational curses.

See dads, you do have an impact. I keep asking what type of impact would you like to have on your daughters? Life and death lie in the power of the tongue so encourage your daughter in every aspect of her life. Allow your little girls the privilege of seeing you treat women respectfully starting with your mother but especially their mother. This is sure to support good decision-making in your daughters' future relationships with men. Otherwise, she may be misguided. I know this from my own personal life experiences.

Misguided behavior on your behalf could encourage your daughter to run to the arms of any man, and sometimes the worst men, please believe me. You have the ability as a father to provide your daughter with the model for a good relationship, since her first real relationship with a man comes through you, her daddy. Bad memories, bad choices, and hard lessons along the way can all be avoided with a guiding touch from a girl's father, starting with her flesh-and-blood father. A daughter has to be introduced to her heavenly father although God is the best father for us all.

I realize the correlation between my father's parents, their disconnected relationship with each other, and the relationships their son built or failed to build. In fact, if you hadn't already predicted that my father's parents had poor relationships with their fathers, you should have. I'm not here to dishonor my grandmother, but to recognize the breakdown. Realizing helps me to avoid repeating these failures and to leave a different legacy behind, and it can help you too.

    At sixteen, my father left for the Northeast to join his mother and eventually the United States Military. His first job was at a hospital where he met his future wife, my mother. Shortly after they met, he joined the military, where he served for six years as an Aircraft and Helicopter Service Technician. Unfortunately, he said, his military career didn't end before he was sent to Vietnam for thirteen months. I don't recall being told about any fond memories of Vietnam or any of his war stories at all for that matter. That's a chapter of his life he never discussed. When asked, he only suggested that there was nothing to tell of his stint in the Marines worth sharing. I would have been intrigued as a child to learn about some of the things he encountered while in the military. He never afforded us, his children, this opportunity if he shared anything, that often though. Perhaps he felt this was best. Truthfully, if only painful memories exist for him, I respect his decision not to do so.

    One wonders. I do recall him sharing one consistent memory for my father about the war he served in: sadness. The sadness for the helpless civilian victims of the war was often too much to bear, he said. As I see it now, my father was probably suffering from post-traumatic stress disorder, leaving a family to deal with a Vietnam Vet with no ammunition fighting through memories that could kill a soldier.

The once-upon-a-time happy couple, my parents, had their first two children after my father returned from the war and then married. Remarkably, during a recent conversation, he said, "I never really felt loved by your mom." What a note-to-self this was. The obvious denominator in this equation was that neither of the two was aware of what God said about this marriage-to-be or, if so, neither spoke of what God said about their marriage to be.

They were feuding even before the wedding, and yes as I've recalled more than once, they probably never should have embarked on a life together as husband and wife. Yes, I realize without them there'd be no me, but rather than all of this heartache, let me ask: What path would have been easier? Take this as a lesson that a couple needs a God-centered foundation prior to becoming man and wife. They need to be whole and complete in God *prior* to their marriage. It is a sad fact that nowadays divorce statistics are high even in the Christian community. However, believers realize that God is able to do all things if they are willing (*Matthew 19:26*).

More importantly, each individual needs a personal relationship with God himself regardless of marital status. I see individual salvation as an added benefit prior to marriage. I have witnessed the power of God in a relationship that developed into a marriage and the many benefits of having it early on. We need salvation from our Lord and Savior Jesus Christ. With that comes the grace to proactively take time to live holy so that innocent children don't come into an unsaved household where two people aren't living pure, whole, and holy for God. It is a recipe for disaster when the parents haven't consulted God about marriage or about the spouse-to-be and have taken the liberty to procreate in sin.

Realistically speaking from this experience, I see this type of inherited problem as the curse of sin. Physical and mental abuse that has taken place in the household cannot be passed down to the next generation. To know better is to do better. As I ponder the family genogram, we all have had children outside of wedlock and lived unholy most our adult lives. Please note this as a lesson; if you do not clearly understand these words, don't pass down ungodliness to your children! If so, you are only being selfish and clearly not considering the repercussions of your daily lives and daily actions. Read about generational curses versus to generational blessings in the Bible (*Exodus 20:5-6*).

By 1979, my parents' marriage had fallen apart due to infidelity that resulted in a child being born outside of marriage to my father. The child came into the world unbeknownst to my mother and she was told by my father that he was not going to deny his son. He would blame my mom for his affair citing that she continually threatened to divorce him.

In the same conversation, admitted that the marriage was doomed as a result of his efforts. He did acknowledge that mom was innocent and came from a good home where her parents were married and acknowledged that her parent's union was blessed from the beginning. It's wonderful to know that one side of my roots kept the marriage covenant from the start. This gives me hope to know that marriage is the lineage I will inherit opposed to a life of sin and fornication from the beginning.

When I asked him about his perception of his aunts, sister and daughter…well, let's just say that it's fair to say he doesn't have a positive image of many women. According to him, all but one aunt were "promiscuous baby-making women." With powerful emotional depth in his voice, he stated, "<u>Don't open your womb anymore to a demon</u>."

His reason for saying so is that if the man is not my husband then, in essence, I'm opening my legs to the devil. This seems to be one place where we agree, and I have followed through with this and kept my word. God didn't call Eve to be a baby mama, a casual sexual encounter, a girlfriend giving away her jewels, or a one night stand creating babies, and God has not called me to be one either (*Matthew 7:6*).

Taking inventory of my father's family history, the history of his sisters and his mother, my father stressed that I should get married so that the blessing of God would be on the union beforehand. He did honor one of his sisters, my Aunt Oli, for being married, along with one of his aunts, Aunt Iri, as well as his grandmother. These few women he holds respect for, but he said he doesn't like the image the other promiscuous family members portray. Over the years, he has alluded to and made certain, that I too, am not excluded from this portrayal.

Spiritually, my father grew up believing in Catholicism. He learned how to worship as a Baptist when he married my mother. Once the family split, he began practicing Islam and adopted a Muslim lifestyle for nearly seven years. When he later remarried after the divorce of my parents, I praise God that he has since found Christ and became a Christian.

From then on is when he earned his nickname, "Walking Bible." His newfound love for the Word earned him the moniker. During a conversation, one of the fondest memories he shared came during his first birthday party, at the age of 50. He was grateful and happy at the time since I decided to host this party in honor of him. Being his oldest child, I thought it'd be a good idea.

We are surprised that my dad credits himself as being a good father. We are not here to steal his joy or discredit his image of his fatherhood but, as his children, we aren't sure what could have brought on such the conclusion. In other words, we don't understand why he would think such a thing when we all felt that he missed a lot of landmarks in our lives, felt he wasn't very supportive, and could have done things differently. There are mixed emotions but consistent feelings and memories associated with a lot of pain from our childhood. We realize no one is perfect and have since come to terms with that.

The opportunity to speak with my dad during his interview for this sake gave me a new point of view about how and why he did some of the things that he did. His negative perception of his broken home early in life lead to a break down in his procreated family with wife and kids which says a lot. He credits his mother for ruining his life and the lives of his siblings early on. He has rejected his father and rarely speaks of him so again, broken pieces of a family from the start.

Fathers, what type of upbringing do you have that sends messages to your little girls? Do you spend time with your own mother? Do you have sisters that you occasionally see, visit, with or even lend a hand to? These are the kinds of things us little girls that grow up to be women want and need in our lives. Show your daughters that not only are they a priority but the other women in your lives are as well. It's so unfair when a man pays so much attention to a love interest but lacks the will to talk to or spend time with his own daughter, mother, sister, etc.

There are three women who I've come to know that my father respects: his former Pastor, Loretta; his cousin, Felicia, who I was named after; and his deceased aunt, Iri. Other than that, the relationships he's held with other women have not been honorable in my view. The ugly part of this is that none of these women he holds in high regard are his mother, his sisters, or either of his wives. Yes, not even his own daughter, me, his only daughter.

Here's why I say I don't see him admiring me: one of his statements that continually returns to me is, "I wish I would have never met your mother because then I wouldn't have you kids." Or better yet: "I don't care about you kids or what you all do." As a child I wasn't strong enough to endure such words. For years my soul felt shattered, and confused that someone like my father, who was supposed to love me, could say such things. This is probably at the core of the reasons why I feel as I do now about gripping the hand of God in the course of so many broken pieces in my heart. What I've learned to do, thank God, is to pray for my father, myself and hurting family. I prayed that God would allow our hearts to purge the hurt and pain so that we could then walk continuously in freedom. I pray you too will have this freedom, as well as your family, if you desire it.

"All money is not good money," my father often says. I take this quote to mean that we should not accept money from just anyone. My father thinks this because he's come to understand that the Bible says that we should be the lender and not the borrower (*Proverbs 22:7*). I would highly agree. The Bible does tell us that the borrower is slave to the lender, and I've learned this lesson for myself. I think money ties many to bondage and I've become strategically careful in not accepting it from just any place or anyone.

I learned to never ask or need to ask my father for anything. The many times leading up to my newness felt very different. I remember many times as a child being the appointed child after the divorce to make the "needs" phone call only to be shattered and rejected to help. Help us three children needed from an able father. So you see I've come to my bridge over deep waters. For me this bridge I cross says I can no longer swim in deep water with him anymore emotionally drowning. Drowning by asking for help is just not worth the effort so I keep things simple, polite, and surface enough to be cordial. Daughters, I encourage you to believe that things can get better, it has for me. It's called boundaries. Through prayer, Godly guidance, wisdom and God will dictate your method of protection. I've surrendered to God on the matter; God helps me often and gives freely without me asking.

      Regarding my mother, he says, "Her body was broken from bad blood." She had to have a spinal tap to diagnose a condition, and I too had to have a spinal tap a few years ago to confirm a condition that was ailing my body. As I listened to him discuss my mother's illness, I could only think just how much life can come full circle. It's amazing how much you can discover about your father when you simply have a conversation with him and listen. Listen for reasons, conclusions, and answers to why he too may be hurt. Hurt, from never releasing anger, frustration, rejection, and the like from the same thing, being or feeling as if he were a fatherless child.

      Fathers, I say this again: health and wholeness is what you want to leave your children, not hurt, disgust, confusion, and pain. If you are a father and grew up fatherless, don't make your daughter pay by not being there for her. Know that all of your children need you.

"They run, they run, and they run," my father always says. Here he'd be, telling me just how much his children run from him. I'll admit I learned to run from the verbal blows. As a result, I grew up running from similar relationships. Can you blame me?

Damaging talk would surround often subjects such as the distaste of their divorce, my mother and his dislike for the process of divorce, child support, lies, etc. of course his displeasing feelings for my siblings. At some point I recognized that my own self-care hinged on me doing something about listening to such toxic talk. I would eventually stop accepting this toxic venom, interject and speak back truth to many distorted non-truths about our family due to his ill will perception. I really don't understand why my mother, who I don't think he ever really got over, or other siblings often become our sole subject matter when we talk. What makes my father think I'd rather listen to him bash my family, instead of hearing a lesson on life? Rather, why did he never take the time to teach me what to do when men try to physically force themselves one me? Talk to me about *rape*! This is what he could have been telling me, how to keep from being *molested* at an early age by a family member or even a neighbor. What about how to fight back when being beaten by men (four in my lifetime). That's something daddy could have been talking to me about.

Fathers, *talk to your daughters*. Must she learn these things the hard way? Must she learn by crying her eyes out, by being vulnerable, by being subjected to such pain, only because you didn't tell her what to do? More often than not, my conversations with my father during my formative years were empty chatter, full of let downs that have transpired throughout his lifetime. What lessons will your daughter have to learn because you are talking to her, but about the wrong things?

Come on dads, have real talk with her. I mean, *really talk to her*, in ways that will help her, in ways that will prevent her from having to see what I've seen. If and when the moment comes and she's put in a situation that could result in rape, molestation, or physical abuse, your words of wisdom will be what could save your little girl.

The alternative is to be like other fathers I know and not talk to your daughter about real issues; watch her on the news, read about her in the newspaper, or see her at the food stamp office, WIC office, or welfare office trying to get help. This is real, fathers! Why do homes have to be fatherless? You have the power to stop it. Be who God has called you to be so this ugly cycle stops. Put an end to the generation-to-generation downward spirals and cycles we see played out in the lives of many children in homes, communities and neighborhoods alike. Doing otherwise is almost like pushing your little princess down a flight of steps while she is still a little baby in her stroller! Something tells me that once you catch a visual of her falling down a flight of steps you really don't want to do that to little princess.

As I recall our conversations I've had with my father, he often asks, "Does that make sense," as if to want validation for pointing out everyone else's issues but his own. And I admit that I would nod my head just to keep the conversation flowing. Is this wrong? You bet. Never justify the wrongs of others. Rather, speak the truth in love even if we realize that your loved one, particularly a parent, is wrong.

As I'm listening, he goes on to say, "Your mother is so sad." He thinks she should call him to talk about the kids, but she refuses to talk to him at all. In her defense, we are not kids anymore. Why would she call the man who was abusive and didn't treat her right? Considering their history, clearly her going forward without him seems reasonable.

This belief that my mother should be reaching out to him signals a certain hope in him, but also reveals his denial. He goes on to say that she lives in mess, running back and forth over money and that she only calls us kids only when she needs something. "She wouldn't even send my kids to my mother's funeral," he says. Although I vividly remember when my paternal grandmother passed, when I was fourteen, I also remember being unaware of how I could arrange for my two brothers and me to attend her funeral hundreds of miles away. I remember feeling guilty for not being able to go.

Could this have been because I was in denial and did not realize that my father should have been the one making these arrangements? Yes it was bizarre since again, I simply redirected the responsibility from an able bodied parent, my dad, to make such arrangements for his three children. My mother was busy raising us children, with very limited support from him. This seems common in America though so our story is similar in nature to countless others. However, it does not have to be. You change the course of your story, your children's stories by being different in a positive way. God will bless you and your seeds. This I know is a guarantee.

"Yeah you need to write a book," my father tells me. The real purpose of this book is to spread knowledge that will help other families that have seen what we've seen and experienced what we've experienced to overcome their struggles. "Families hide too much s—t," my father says, laughing. You think? Yes, I know this is truth. Hence my reasons for telling this story in an effort to help others live outside the walls of repressed denial.

For the summers, we were sent to live with my father. At the end of one summer, he decided not to send us back home to mom. "Your mother had my support for a long time," he says. "She said she wanted to go to school so I took you kids and told her to go to school." As we've grown, though, we've come to understand that his not returning us home in that fall was a strategy to keep us children in his physical custody and thereby have his child support lawsuit dropped.

Fathers, in the event you are not with the mother of your children any longer, consult an attorney regarding your rights and shared physical and legal custody. If you're using lawsuits for any other reason, you're hurting your children in the long run. They will see through your attempt to avoid being a full-time father dodging child support payments.

The year we spent with my father and without our mother was often uphill battle. I remember thinking as a kid, Dang, I can't wait to go back to live with mother. Although our mother rarely had money or food to feed us, we had peace in the midst of a refined storm. The car was repossessed many times; the electricity, water, and telephone were often disconnected. But we always had the love and support of our good mother.

Cable television was never an option for us when we were children, and making do with less became a normal way of life for us. But because we had love, and a praying mother God the father always stepped in to provide for us. Because our mother was centered on God being the provider, we prevailed. As I think about how my dad grew up, we as his children sometimes lived under similar conditions but not to that extreme. I'm amazed at how a man could assume all of his children's needs were taken care of even if he played a minor part in providing for three children's daily needs. Could it be he just did not think twice about this? Perhaps so.

God helped my mother to keep things together in the midst of the many storms. After the divorce she became an obvious single, but a strong, mother. God was there all along, even if my young mind didn't know who was behind the scenes helping us persevere. I'm forever grateful to our heavenly father.

My father goes on to say how he owes me nothing. "You never sent me any money. Feli never gave me more than $100." How is this man actually comparing what his children have done for him? I've never heard a parent discuss what their children have or have not done for them to them.

Fathers, if you're reading, please don't do this. "I don't ask for anything," my father says, but whether you ask your children for anything or not isn't the issue. The issue becomes the public declaration to your children of what has or has not been done on your behalf as a father. He went on to say how my younger brother had given my mother a lot of money. So what? I'm actually not surprised by the assistance my mother received; she was left carrying the burden of caring for four children, three of which were his with little to no financial support of either of the fathers.

Once we became adults, my father was ordered to pay overdue child support. Father's child support is an obligation for you to help financially raise your children. It is not a paycheck for the mothers, separate the two and be financially responsible to your children in that manner. Also declaring what you've paid is not doing anything to help your kids feel better about your efforts. You and God know what you've done and, believe me, child support records are public records, so you need not declare your financial responsibility to your children to anyone.

"How's she going to love you, and hurt me in that way?" He asks me of my mother, but I see no connection between my mother's love for her children and joint payments from her former husband for the children he fathered. His question clearly comes from a mentality of victimization.

Fathers, please take responsibility and know that child support and your relationship with the mother of your children are two altogether different matters. Separate your thoughts about a woman you may resent for leaving you; your children need your financial help. When you're withholding assistance because of your dislike for your children's mother, you're punishing your children. It goes back to a false idea I've heard about paying tithes to a local church: "I'm not paying money to make the pastor rich." Your support is not about the pastor, though, nor is your child support about the mother's name on your check. God sees all and knows all, so leave it in his hands and do what's right for your children. What they do beyond you paying your share is out of your control. You could continue trying to control these matters, but in the long run not paying tithes or child support will have a lasting effect, a detrimental effect on you, your children, and your faith.

Unfortunately in our society, it seems as if the legal effects of marriage outlast the God-given benefits of marriage. One example would be children inheriting the last name of their father. In my dad's case, though, I have to wonder if it was a blessing to inherit his father's name, since he only saw him once in his lifetime. This is the case for many children, and the name gives them a constant reminder of their father, but without the time and the financial or emotional benefits. Bearing the name of an absent father can be a detrimental reminder of the non-existing relationship but it is right. Some disagree and I certainly can't argue their point since it is the responsibility of the father and husband to lead the family.

My siblings and I feel as if we have no one's name at this point, since my father changed his last name after he was divorced from my mother many years ago. Only his children still have his former name and one from a grandfather we never met or knew. Would you therefore say I have an unknown last name? I would, and in discussing this with my dad, he's not even sure if the name I grew up with really is his father's last name. You see fathers, there's a lot in a name. Take a moment to consider this, too. I once wondered why my grandmother would give the name of an absent father to a child or one she isn't sure truly exist. What was the advantage? My grandfather to this day has never acknowledged my father as his son.

"Does that make sense," my father keeps asking in the recorded interview, and I agree with him like a kid who's afraid to get in trouble. Covering for my father's lies has become so habitual; an obvious of being ashamed to be honest with him at that point. I was unable to withstand being further tormented by disagreeing. For years I'd agree with his rhetorical questions even though I felt he was wrong and knew inside it wasn't right to simply agree when I truly disagreed within. Now, I no longer walk in fear with him nor do I agree when he asks, "Does that make sense." Especially if it simply does not make sense to me.

Father's please note this isn't positive communication, when you manipulate your kids into agreeing with you, especially when you are wrong and you know it. Allow them the independence of sharing their voice with you in a healthy conversation. Otherwise, don't ask them for their input if you are only going to use the information as a weapon against them. This was the case with my father, and despite the fact that I no longer will agree blindly with him, it still is a weapon, any form of input on my behalf. I truly believe better communication between us is possible because I believe in God. This is my hope for you too. (See *2 Tim 2:23)*

Before grandma died he said he talked to my grandmother, trying to find out about her life, and thereby his own life, once he became an adult. I see parallels between my grandmother's life and the way my life went as a young woman. What is most important is that history *shall not* repeat itself. Through these eyes I have seen a lot and, really, while it may hurt to know the truth of your family it could also empower you. Don't be afraid to confront the generational curses or deformities within your family. Knowledge is power, so confront them head on. God gives us love, power and sound minds to do so (*2 Tim 1:7*).

Interview your parents so that you too will know what legacy you *do not* intend to leave to your own children. For me I declare it will not be bi-polar disorder, depression, infidelity, lust, promiscuity, illegitimate children or divorce. None of these are of God. Instead fathers declare blessings over your families, especially over your little girls. They need you to.

Because I wanted a better understanding of my family heritage, I made a point to visit my father's native country. It was an out-of-body experience. To see poverty on the level that exists in Central America was quite overwhelming but to embellish in such a beautiful place was heart- warming at the same time. On the other hand, this valuable experience provided answers to questions about his childhood. It was very interesting to see the school he attended as a child and the very building they lived in.

What stuck with me the most was the room, the single room; all his siblings, mother, and grandmother lived in. Can you imagine the room you're sitting in now being occupied by several other people all together? These types of things happen when children are born into relationships without the covenant of God, or relationships that result in children being raised in single parent households.

Fathers, you are respectfully known as the bread winners. We appreciate this but please be there, not just financially, but by spending time with your children. If you sense or see that the mother is unable on any level, care enough to provide a better life for your children, even if that means becoming the full-time parent and provider.

In the case of my grandmother, I often wonder whether she knew her worth, knew whose child she really was, or even if she knew her heavenly father. If she had, maybe life would have been different for her as well as her children. As her granddaughter, I see that unless I confronted myself on these matters, my life could have very easily resembled hers.

My father bragged about how his grandmother taught him to be the messenger in the family. Maybe she was one of the few women he honored, too. He had been assigned as the grandchild that went to the store with a list of eight or nine items to remember to bring home. He was ordered not to write these items down in an effort to build his memory, he says. I often wonder, with such a good memory, how he hardly ever remembers my birthday. He always calls on the day before but never the date *if* he calls. I guess early rather than never is better? That's a question I often struggle with since I realize in life we are able to set standards and priorities for those we deeply care for. At least he calls, some would argue. On the other hand, he wasn't present during my birth, so it would make a lot of sense for him not to know my birthday, or not to care. This is of course all my perceptions and an easy assumption since he's never declared otherwise.

My father didn't attend high school or graduate from a four-year college. As an adult, I can now clearly see why he may not have treasured the day I graduated from either high school or the universities I attended. Although naïve that he'd come, one of the most disappointing things was the high school graduation he did not attend. For someone to treasure your success, I'd imagine they'd have to remember the strength it took to achieve similar success. He didn't attend and I was simply crushed on a day when I should have been bearing all smiles. Fathers, make your children feel validated. It does matter when you became a parent; now that you are, it's no longer just about you.

Surprisingly, my father says in one of our talks for the sake of this book that we were very good kids. We migrated from the North to the South in the late 1970s. He says, "N. decided to move south. Ya'll were very good kids, very well mannered." We think, as his children, that we still are, but why then did we hear so often from him, while we were growing, that we weren't?

"In 1979," he says, "everything fell apart. The family fell apart after my confession of infidelity." My mother couldn't handle it, and I can't say I blame her. "Scripture says you have what you say and she kept crying divorce," he says. He admitted that my mother only started loving him after she discovered the affair. This profound statement has taken me back to a place where I'd ask myself, what type of nonsense is this? If the cause of the divorce was infidelity, how did she amazingly find a newfound deep sense of love for him? Knowing my mother and her side of the story, I can't help but think this is untrue.

On the other hand, I've heard of couples who started wrong and made things right, became stronger and persevered in their marriage beyond indiscretions. No matter the situation, two people who really want to make the marriage work can do it. In my parents' marriage I don't think this was the case. The indiscretions and abuse were too much. I watched the affair destroy two families. According to my father, his mistress was married to a man that was incarcerated for some time. I can imagine the vulnerability she felt because her husband was away in prison, and on drugs, according to what he's said. I can only imagine what was going through her mind when she met my dad, who in fact can be very charming.

I've read the Commandment myself (*Exodus 20:4*), and realize that the children of the cursed father are of the third and fourth generations. It's always been my understanding that the generational curses or iniquities of the father will be revisited through his children if he isn't obedient by honoring the commandments. My suggestion is to seek your Bible for an exact understanding. As a man, when you honor

God and obey his Commandments, your lineage of a thousand generations will inherit blessings (*Exodus 20:5-6*). Wouldn't you rather your children and a thousand generations beyond your children, be blessed?

My dad reflected on the interesting behavior of his grandfather, but only briefly. He spent more time visiting the idea of what he witnessed in the lives of the surrounding women who raised and reared him than on the men in his life. This was very interesting. It seems more of his frustrations came from women than from men, but his father was not there. The women were there to rear him as many single mothers and probably should be honored. It takes forgiveness and admiration to honor those who were at least there to carry on the affairs of those who simply do not meet their responsibility as parents.

My dad told me that my grandmother, his mother, died waiting for a specific man to marry her. Sadly, this man never did. What a disappointment to her! She was in love with a man who had a sick wife but my grandmother died before they could get together. I see myself in this behavior. I, too, once made the decision to wait on a man who was not physically available to me, not that he was married to a sick wife but in the midst of the scenario, found it eye opening to see the kernel of my own decision to wait in my grandmother's actions. In the end, it isn't worth the wait. Live your life now and leave the waiting to God and his timing. Ladies I say this with depth because I know. Learn from it but leave it alone and move on.

I truly believe it takes a big person to admit fault when they know they're the cause of a divorce, but I don't think my father has ever confessed this to my mother that their divorce was his fault. He did years later ask her for forgiveness after becoming a Christian. Men, would you fess up and ask for forgiveness provided this scenario was yours? It's sad but true that many never will or do. We crumbled as a result of infidelity in the marriage. As I listen to him describe the devastating divorce, I can actuality sense one of the reasons in addition was the pride of my dad.

See *Deuteronomy 28:2* for a lesson on sweat-less blessings. Pondering life experiences, I clearly see through these eyes how his life has been a clear learning experience. My prayer is that the rest of his life on Earth will be the best life he can live. We don't always agree but, after all, he is still my father.

When referring to one of the aunts that reared him, he recalled how her husband neglected her. He went on to say that, "Her own children didn't show her love and affection either." Perhaps they were simply mimicking what they had seen with their father, being an emotionless being while living under the same roof. For that reason he stated that her children (his cousins) "didn't show love and affection to their spouses or children either." Here's that generational curse mentioned earlier, caused by the sins of the father. It's rumored my great aunt actually died from a broken heart due to the actions of her not-so-great husband.

Fathers, it is vital that you are there no matter the circumstances. Absenteeism isn't acceptable, although it may be more convenient for you. If you want your children to be well-rounded and to develop healthy, well-balanced relationships, make the effort to nurture. Your time is necessary for this to occur. Can this be done without your presence as a father? Maybe, but more likely not. Children were never intended to come into the world to be raised by one person. Remember the older generations understood that it takes a village to raise a child. I concur.

My father went on to discuss how his sisters have gone from man to man, "with their big behinds having babies like their mother." What a thing to say about your own family; that's a declaration I could never make about my own family. Even if my grandmother's legacy to him indicates she lived up to being a woman who didn't treasure herself, she still does not deserve to be remembered in such a way. She passed when I was only fourteen, and I've recently come to realize how much I wish she were here for me to know her.

My take away from my father's memory of grandmother is that I must surpass the legacy of being a single mother of several illegitimate children. I've learned from her example. I will admit, however, to seeing the generational resemblances, since I too have been known for my big behind. I can honestly admit I resemble her in some respects, especially the way I stand and the way I walk. Based just on the few fond memories and the handful of pictures I have of her, I largely resemble her.

I can't help imagine how men go for the women with the big behind and then leave behind the seeds of life they plant, their children. Fathers, please help me to understand the thought process that allows you to disconnect from your children as a result of your disconnection with their mother. This was the case with my grandmother, my aunts, and even his own daughter, all of whom have given birth to children out of wedlock. The funny thing is not only do we all physically resemble each other, but we also resemble each other in the choices we've made. I chalk this up to the single parent households where we were raised. My thought is that men can leave us behind in the dust, as if they have no memory of the women beyond the flesh. I presume that they lack the desire to raise their seed because they have no heart or simply just don't care enough to do so. An alternative view would lend itself to say that the fatherless will do that father-less.

Interestingly, my father said our choice of men left us women behind with babies and nothing to show for our time, effort, and energy but the knowledge of having been used as sex objects. In our family, there are more unmarried granddaughters with babies than there are wives with babies. We can turn this around though. I believe that with God, as clearly stated in the Word, all things are possible (*Matthew 19:26*). It starts with our individual actions.

One thing I think my father fails to realize is that we did not impregnate ourselves. Men did. This is a perfect time for you fathers of precious daughters to teach them the value of being a wife instead of a "baby mama." Trust me; the talk could in essence change the course of their lives. Your input is valuable. Not to have this talk with your little girl, even if she's an adult, is detrimental. You see, dads, we all know your secret: she's always going to be your little girl. That being the case, please have the self-worth talk with her so she'll avoid the infamous and disrespectful title of "baby mama."

Fathers, don't compare your children in front of one another. Doing so silently, in your own head, is one thing, but openly comparing your children isn't a positive thing. It negatively triggers the child's self-esteem and makes them feel they are always trying to live up to the example of another, not realizing that God made each child special, unique, and a peculiar person (*1 Peter 2:9*).

From what I gathered during our talk, my father's perception of me is that I didn't listen to him early in life. Although he's sharing his honest feelings, I'm steady pondering my own thoughts and asking myself but why should I have been listening to him when most of what he says sounded so distasteful when I was growing up? He says, "Now you're living by the Gospel because you don't agree with just anything that I say." The Word tells us not to listen to Godless chatter (*2 Timothy 2:16*), so some things I retain and others I dismiss when he says something that does not line up with my inner spirit. Remember he said "do not open your womb to another fallen demon." We agree, but unfortunately, this comes many years too late. I have made this mistake but I also realize that we are to remain teachable.

Fathers, we need you to be dads and really, really speak to your daughters about life. It also isn't a bad idea to support her dreams. Please don't father by default; be a dad by design. He went on to tell me that right now in my life, "What's saving you is that you have respect for your parents. You have a relationship with your mother." If your parents would just come together," he says, "you'd be able to get married overnight. If only your parents could talk." The thing is my eternal Father, God, and my mother does talk. She's a praying mother and one who talks to God the Father often, practically every day. I have to admit that having a blessing from both my parents would be nice, but having the approval of a man is no longer a necessity for me. Rather, knowing for me who to marry and when to marry him is essential. More importantly, my heavenly Father will let me, His daughter; know when it is time to marry. Don't misinterpret that I'm above my parent's blessing for such a lifelong commitment but I've come to understand that God approves before man does.

"You're just like your mother," my father says. "You use the word 'no' like an inherited weapon." It's this little word, he says, that caused an affair that resulted in a child outside of their marriage. I had never before thought about how the word "no" in a marriage could turn into a weapon, but I can sympathize in theory with this idea just a little. However, it that was the case, then the word "no" throughout their marriage was an apparent for a reason. Satan is busy enough without me helping him along the way in my marriage-to-be.

Sometimes I use to think I was resentful. Why so? I guess because for the most part my father has not been the "daddy" I've needed all my life. In discovering my heavenly purpose, thankfully I've discovered the Father of many fathers, the Daddy of all daddies: God.

Let's be real though. I needed my flesh-and-blood father in many areas of my life but have come to realize not having him left me feeling broken, un-affirmed, unaccepted, and neglected on many accounts. Fathers, when you look at your little pumpkin's face, can you imagine her feeling the same as a result of your negligence, absence, lack of support and the like? Let me guess: no. Look at little pumpkin's picture again, but this time picture her being a well-developed, balanced and fruitful child that will grow up to be the finest young lady that you'd want to be proud of. The latter option can be as a result of your love, support and influence in a positive manner.

My father went on to say, "Your mother was very kind to me." For some reason, this seems in a direct conflict with what he says about her on a regular basis. Being honest, it's kind of hard to hear him say that she was kind to him while knowing he despises her at times. At least, that's the impression I get when he spoke of her in ill-will, so when he says something nice, I kind of struggle with believing he means it. It's the same way I feel when he says things that are nice and kind about me. You can get side tracked with the flipped personality. One day nice, next day mean.

      On the other hand, my mother gave him three children and weathered more than a number of storms in the household. She gave him thirteen-plus years of her life and many years she gave involuntarily as she tried to get beyond her bitterness, pain, anger, frustration, and un-forgiveness. She gave a lot. Probably more than she realized she would when she first met my father. Had she known, I'm guessing her decision would have been different. For this reason, I think we should more often look at the signs prior to marriage. Proactive is better than reactive. What I mean by "signs" is that you should look at your partner to determine if you can be together forever. Self-assess and evaluate your feelings. They are generated from somewhere. More than often that still small inner voice inside is God prompting us to pay attention to his cues, clues and signs to halter, ponder, and flat out turn in the opposite direction. If you cannot see that person in your life in a vision down the road, seventy years later, you may want to rethink wasting your productive time with someone destined to be another's spouse since you don't see them as yours. This is just an opinion, but the divorce statistics seem to agree that more revelation is necessary and needed when considering marriage.

What I should have asked my father was what he contributed to each of his marriages. I never asked what he felt he contributed. Fathers, have you taken inventory of what you've contributed to your children, the mother of your children, or even your wife? Are you a taker or a giver in relationships? Whatever the case, today is your chance to change whatever behaviors you don't like that you're seeing. Let God guide you in this matter; He is a wonderful GPS system.

Another thing fathers: do you take your family to church or do you send your family to church? Take them; don't send them, to church. You are the head of the household, not the tail of the household and you hold a lot of rank within your family. In fact, your wife and children really look up to you whether you realize it or not. Whether your family actually says that they look up to you or not, they probably do. In talking over the years with many women, they desire to look up to their husbands, not down. Take your rightful place and don't let Satan create illusions that say otherwise.

My father says that, "As a child, I went to church, but only for the purposes of having food to eat." He says, "We weren't connected to God and didn't know the Bible. As a child, I went to no one's church. I only went for Christmas and Easter and to eat since we were hungry at home. I had no clothes to go to church."

This has been the case for many but it does not have to be the case for you or your family.

    For me as a little girl, Harvest Baptist Church was our first family church. Although I liked it, we didn't last long there. What I mean is that we started going to church as a family, but not for long. I can vaguely remember us attending as a family, usually only my mom and other siblings. That was probably the beginning of the end for our family and we didn't realize it. I can even recall how I was introduced to Jesus Christ and God at Harvest Baptist Church. That's where I recall accepting Christ as my Lord and Savior and being baptized as a young child for the first time. If memory serves me clearly, I was eight years old.

    Perhaps my flesh-and-blood father didn't understand the essence of being the head of the family at that time because of his rearing and lack of true faith. Instead, he exuded the defiant attitude of one who'd rather not indulge in something as unfamiliar as in going to church for worship service. I sensed from our later conversations that going to church was something he could live without then. If it could be done all over again, I highly doubt if either parent would take the approach of not serving God as a young family. Knowing both my parents now and their walk with Christ, I think they'd agree.

    Fathers, whatever your beliefs are—and I hope you're saved believers—share them with your children. The best inheritance you can leave for your children is salvation. It's worth more than any tangible item on

Earth. Gird their foundation from an early age by making them members of a saved family. The world offers many temptations and things to stunt the growth of the family, and without the guiding, leading love of God, you are defenseless. I know this now but because our family had little foundation from the start, we were severely stunted. Dad agrees.

    I remember my mother stating how she wanted to get premarital counseling from the church and he wasn't willing. Wow, another stunt from the very start. Why not employ the aid of a skillful counselor who could have very well detected the need for change early on which may have expanded the years of our family life. If I were a Life Coach, just based on errors, trials, and temptations, I'd suggest that a man become fully aware of his confidence in Christ before becoming a husband and, especially, a father. I feel a man doesn't really know who he is without gaining confidence in Christ or his God given purpose. Another thing that I've learned from friendships and conversations with men is that they've hitched their sense of security to many of the material things of the world: cars, homes, titles, money, etc. Oftentimes, they ignore the Word and what God has to say to them. I've learned the hard way that men who are still searching for their identity will follow anything that sounds soothing or fits their lifestyle. Fathers, is this you? I encourage you to explore an honest answer to this question.

    My father became a Muslim in the late 1980s. His influence convinced us to change our last name for a year to one that reflected his Islamic faith. He loves his Islamic name and has kept it, even though he denounced the religion when he came to Christianity. Evidently, he realized that this religious practice, created by man, dishonored the rights of women and left it. Islam also accepts men taking more than one wife, something he says he doesn't agree with. I thank God, and so does he, for coming to terms with denouncing such practices, accepting the name of Jesus as his Savior and going on with his life without looking back.

In his final words during our talk my father stated, "I love my children and think that I was a good father. I've never been a bad father. Your mother always had a daddy; I never had that."

Do you see what I see? I truly think my father has his own definition of what is considered being a "good" father; he was emotionally unavailable, provided a negative example for marriage, and failed to create relationships with his children. What I see is that we still need to build solid relationships within the family and this starts with him, our head. His children, who have now become adults, don't always indulged him with time due to everyone's own lives or with each other and have at times become distant strangers. We'd credit more than a portion of our failed knack to soundly communicate, connect in a positive manner clearly a result of the hurtful things he said to us as we were growing up.

We have moved on and since forgiven him though. Yes, we have to forgive, but remember this is the opposite of forgetting. Even if you try, the hurt still lingers and runs deep. Fathers, accept your rightful place in your families lives so that this is not your story being shared with the world especially if it isn't in the best of fashion in your opinion. If not, you too may negatively influence your children's futures. Lasting remarks make a profound difference and leave a lasting impression. Which do you prefer your children to have of you, good thoughts or indifferent, resentful thoughts?

Change, repent, and forgive. Yes, forgive yourself and seek better for you and your children.

Chapter 3
Fatherless Statistics

What he felt as a man, a father, and a former husband to my mom—was included in this book so that I could gather a better understanding of *his* view of being a father, one that we needed. Knowing firsthand how he thought, how he felt and perceived himself as a father was essential. Again, this published experience isn't being used as a tool to tear men down, it's just a recounting to help you see what daughter's see, especially when they are not afforded a healthy relationship from the start with their daddy.

I do however believe as one of my favorite pastors says: "How you start is not how you finish." With that in mind, I am hopeful that this has helped you in some way. Know that this uncomfortable time in your life, the terrible memories, will pass. In other words, "this too shall pass" and healing is on its way.

Talking with my paternal father really helped me to see his side of the story and really gave me the clarity I needed to understand him so that I could help others see a path to fruitful father-daughter relationships. I have a feeling that women would make better choices in romantic relationships with men as a result of healthier relationships with their dad.

Again, it was an attempt to be civil and to, more importantly, create a way to talk through some of the issues that have robbed us of being a family that led me to asking my father for his perspective on things as they transpired. You may be led to do the same in your family. I hope so.

As we know from statistics on fatherless households, how many people are using a lack of communication as an excuse for mediocre relationships with your children when you have the ability to be greater? There are manifold benefits to pursuing a better relationship with your children. For the children out there, there are bounties to be had for pursuing a better relationship with your parents. Both fathers and daughters need to consider the cost of maintaining healthy relationships. Society is hard on men but, in the eyes of children, they could care less how society sees their fathers. Whether he's the world's worst employee, an inmate, or living in another state, children want a father's love, time, affection, and support, and they never *stop* needing it! They don't just want a father's last name, or his home, or his car; they need *dads*! They need real fathers to be there regardless and they need a father's time. Quality time.

Many would say that my father never had a fair chance. Perhaps, but I honestly feel like he made choices when he was unsupportive and verbally abusive to me, my mother, and my siblings. The genogram and his own admission demonstrated that he lacked positive male role models in his own childhood. As a studying clinician, I understand the notion that a supportive father needs to have been a supported son himself beforehand. Without the chance to have a good father to lead and guide him, he was presented with more challenges. But don't forget about the father-son role models we all share: Jesus Christ and God the Father. When God isn't the leading guide in the home, the home is easily a broken one.

Because God designed the family to have a father as a part of the home, there's a great need to have a father's presence in children's lives. For God this is normal and natural, but sadly society's statistics dictate something else.

Fathers, the following research is for *you*. Here are results of your absence in the home. Society, research experts, and statisticians all say that fatherless homes contribute to soaring statistics in alcohol abuse, poverty, teen pregnancies, imprisonment, and many other areas. The number of fatherless households in our society is growing. Having single parent homes, no matter what we see in society, is not normal and creates so many burdens on the one parent playing two roles. "Of children ages 5 to 14, 1.6 million return home to houses where there is no adult present" (Source: U.S. Bureau of the Census, "Who's Minding the Kids?")

So Fathers, when you're considering leaving and not cleaving to your wife or, worse, actually making a child with someone other than your wife, consider your contribution to society's high number of fatherless households. Look around. Take a survey at the park on a Sunday afternoon of how many single mothers you see playing with their children alone. Better still, visit an elementary school any day of the week and see the single mothers dropping children off at school. Fathers, where are you? She did not make this child alone but is now part of a growing number of single parents raising children alone.

Domestic violence statistics have continued to rise rather than decline in our society. Even though women are more likely to be the victim of domestic violence based on research, women are also sometimes responsible for victimizing their spouses; "Battered Men: The Hidden Side of Domestic Violence" reports that 835,000 men are abused each year (batteredmen.com). What about hitting another person in an abusive way is worth it? You have to wonder.

My father seemed more willing to be a man who came and went at his discretion but not a committed husband or father. Come on fathers; let's have a heart to heart. Have a talk with yourself before you commit to a relationship and well before children get involved and you discover that you aren't committed. What you're reading in my own life story is the ripple effect of non-commitment on the level of being the head in the relationship.

Statistics say this all sounds familiar, hence half of marriages ending in divorce: 50% percent of first marriages, 67% of second and 74% of third marriages, according to Jennifer Baker of the Forest Institute of Professional Psychology in Springfield, Missouri. Could it simply be that mate selection, along with not really trusting God for divine connections, is an issue? This question is worth pondering. I see 90% of the issue here being that we prematurely choose what God hasn't approved for us in terms of a mate. I suggest dating, not marrying, that person until you're absolutely sure, and I certainly don't suggest procreating with them unless you're married.

Fathers, I do believe as we mature in life we should do better, especially when we *know* better. I also feel that fathers are the patriarchs of the family and when they aren't visible the family becomes a "headless body". I think if you really realized just how important you are to your families and the success rate of the family, then more families would stay together. Society, experts, and statisticians would be reporting positive numbers, rather than the reverse, especially in the church. 28% of those who attend church regularly have been determined to have lower divorce rates (edivorcepapers.com).

Fathers need to be present in the lives of those who are connected to them. Your children come from you, they are your seed. Please don't contribute to the many fatherless people that roam this world without their foundation.

"Fatherless children are at a dramatically greater risk of drug and alcohol abuse, mental illness…poor educational performance, teen pregnancy, and criminality."

—U.S. Department of Health and Human Services, National Center for Health Statistics

"Fatherless children are at dramatically greater risk of suicide."

—U.S. Department of Health and Human Services

"Boys who grow up in father-absent homes are more likely than those in father-present homes to have trouble establishing appropriate sex roles and gender identity."

—P.L. Adams, J.R. Milner, and N.A. Schrepf

"Compared to peers in two-parent homes, black children in single-parent households are more likely to engage in troublesome behavior, and perform poorly in school."

—Tom Luster and Hariette Pipes McAdoo

"Children with fathers at home tend to do better in school, are less prone to depression and are more successful in relationships. Children from one-parent families achieve less and get into trouble more than children from two parent families."

—"One Parent Families and Their Children: The School's Most Significant Minority," conducted by The Consortium for the Study of School Needs of Children from One Parent Families, co-sponsored by the National Association of Elementary School Principals and the Institute for Development of Educational Activities.

There's more to report beyond these numbers but, the more you study the fatherless children in our society, the worse the statistics get.

You see, fathers, you have a strong position in what you do in the world, so receive your confidence in Christ and be the best dad you can be. Otherwise, do nothing and be responsible for contributing to the aforementioned depressing numbers in society. I applaud those who are contributing and encouraging those who do not. A new day can begin with you today. The decision lies with you. Be the head, not the tail.

As Christians, we should lead by example, so having two parent households in marriage should be our common priority. First and foremost men, be the husband to your wife so that you can be the father to your children in the same household. From my own childhood, I remember only a silhouette of a man, and I hope for better for you.

As a unit, my family has experienced many days of suffering, pain, and resentment that we've continued to hold inside. It was a hidden secret within the walls of each of us, and we didn't share it with others. Even within the family, we barely spoke of our pain, only venting now and then to each other. We wanted to get beyond the pain and the codependent relationships, but we didn't know how back then. We did the best we could to make it through as a torn family.

Since then, in more than one way, each member of the family has had to come to terms with the way they'd choose healing. I remember being so embarrassed about my feelings and wanting to suppress them so badly that my mother, two younger siblings, and I attended family therapy, only for me to deny the help. As a child, I was too shy to discuss my true feelings. It was as if I felt wrong to acknowledge my pain, and I did not confess my feelings to anyone. It was only after learning to pray that I began to unveil my feelings by talking and sharing what's truly in my heart about my experiences with my father.

    Over time we learned to talk about what we each saw, felt, and encountered as a result of our broken family life, both before and after the divorce. We all have come to a much different place to discuss how we each were affected. Amazingly, we now communicate better as a family; we don't withhold feelings from anyone, including our father.

Chapter 4
For Daughters: Is It Abuse?
"Good parents raise good children."

Abused children will do the same: abuse. People who hurt, hurt people in return. When a child grows up adapting to abusive behaviors and language they are being cheated and deceived on the most profound level. Have you taken a moment to ask yourself where you lack in love if you've grown up fatherless? Do an inventory of what ails you in mind or spirit. Were you abused? Have you even considered that you were the victim of abuse? Even verbal abuse is abuse—this is considered emotional abuse.

According to experts, the family is the first institution of learning. "Witnessing violence between one's parents or caretakers is the strongest risk factor of transmitting violent behavior from one generation to the next. Boys who witness domestic violence are twice as likely to abuse their own partners and children when they become adults. 30% to 60% of perpetrators of intimate partner violence also abuse children in the household."

At the same time, you cannot blame parents entirely for the decisions you make in life, especially when you become an adult. My own feeling is that once you know better you tend to do better, so an abusive upbringing doesn't justify wrong actions.

Thank God for being the Father in our lives. Being a Christian provides this benefit, but those who are not yet believers may be lost as a result of a flesh-and-blood father who was abusive or absent, and add to the terrible social statistics. "When my father forsakes me then the Lord will take care of me," the Bible tells us (*Psalms 27:10*).

I remember being told by my mother that dad was not capable of loving another human being. Obviously she felt and had verifiable reasons for feeling as such. I do see my dad as being capable of loving others, however, and for this reason I continue to try to have a civil father-daughter relationship with him. I'd be wrong to encourage you to dismiss your father, as the Bible says we are to honor our fathers. I suggest that you honor him in your own way without harming yourself in the process if your relationship has been toxic.

A dear friend who is a therapist once asked me, "Why subject yourself to abuse for the sake of the other person?" That said, I told myself to continue communicating with my father, but only if it is not harmful for me in mind, or spirit. Although my father never physically abused me, many of the un-forsaken words he spoke to vex my spirit may as well have been punches in the stomach. Even asking myself which would be worse, I can't come up with an answer. Both emotional and physical abuse is bad because they both hurt.

It's just my opinion, but I believe that words hurt more, since physical wounds tend to heal quicker. Ill-spoken words tend to linger and transmit down into your soul, play on your emotions and even speak to an unhealthy self-esteem over time. The choice still lies within you to decide just how long you will allow this to continue. This is easier said than done but very possible. Ask God the father to help you (*Matthew 7:7*).

Where one may hurt you, another one will love you and although many of you daughters may, like me, played out the rejection you felt by entertaining unhealthy relationships, you can be found by a man who can handle your delicate heart and love you purely. I hope you discover this real love, especially that of God.

For me, I had to learn that it's okay to love another purely and it's okay to be loved in return, provided it's a healthy connection and not one that will further damage your fragile heart. My maternal grandparents were married longer than they have lived apart from one another. This often times takes a while but with God all things are possible (*Matthew 19:26*).

The Word tells us that it's not good for man to be alone (*Genesis 2:18*). When you trust yourself to live outside of your pain, your resentment, and your fear of rejection, you can learn to open your heart to receive love. Although you may feel robbed by the hurt and disgust that came from your first relationship with a man—your father—it is still possible to entertain healthy relationships with men. It's true, a daddy should show his daughter how to be treated in a relationship, but for those of you who didn't learn this from your flesh-and-blood father, know that God the Father will show you how you should be treated. The will within you to seek the heavenly Father will help you see the value of replacing the pain in your heart with freedom.

For me, God the Father has and still provides love, vision, direction, and revelation that helps me go forward in my life with or without the sometimes painful relationship with my flesh-and-blood father. Some of the best gifts God could have given me, since I knew nothing about me or who I was, were declaring and confirming my purpose while here on this earth. He gave me confidence in who I am. What I mean by that is that God confirmed I am His child first. Although I may have wandered around feeling unsupported by my father for many years, God has since made up for that. God's love is pure and unconditional and always gives me the assurance that He has my best interests at heart. For this reason, I seek Him. Even when I did not know how to, He was still there covering me along the way.

Like any other parent should, could, or would, my dad always had his own directions, visions, and revelations for my life and how it should go. The odd thing is that even though he's never been here or maybe never knew how to support the dreams I had, his dreams always superseded my own. I think it's only natural to want to be approved by your parents; that need for acceptance is natural. I can honestly say that I always wanted their approval, and at times still need their approval. The difference now is that I seek the guidance and direction from the Heavenly Father first for the okay. That said, doing what dad thought I should do was often times a mission for me, even if it meant ignoring what I felt was my true calling.

    The Word clearly says that we are to follow the vision, direction, and leadership of the heavenly Father, always. His sheep hear and know his voice (*John 10:3-4*). Do you? If not, I encourage you to take the time to get to know God's voice. A wise man once told me that parents are to be the loudest voice in their children's ears. I can recall all those times God's voice said to do this or that and I have since given credit to Him each time his voice told me to do something. He has never led me astray. Because I didn't always make sound choices when I was a child, I thank God for speaking to me. It was always the voice of knowledge, wisdom, and kindness.

    At some point you may need to surrender and listen to the voice of God. You may find fulfillment in knowing his voice is louder than any other voices you'll hear. You too will understand that some of the other voices you hear will become lower until you'll only desire the voice of the Father himself. Of course, God uses other voices—like my mom, respected older friends, aunts, and mentors. He uses people, Rama words from your pastor, and the like to speak to you as well. Godly counsel is the key to your listening.

    Again, this is not to say that you should stop listening to your flesh-and-blood father entirely, but I gather that since you have found this book, you need to know how to leave behind the voice that hinders you, hurls abuse and nonsense to listen instead for the voice of assurance, integrity, and the like. Trust me, I hear you and understand.

What I found is that reading God's Word, praying, and sometimes even fasting make the other voices get smaller. Only then do I learn to be led and stop seeking the approval of others. From God you'll get the okay when there isn't another voice to validate your thoughts, your feelings & your emotions. Who better to confirm your purpose than God? You know that empty feeling you have when you don't know your father? That's because you need your father. In fact, you need both fathers. If your flesh-and-blood father has disappointed you, take me up on the option of praying, forgiving and relinquishing it all to God because he is here!

As time went on, I wondered if my distorted view of relationships would drastically affect the interactions I'd have with men in my future. I didn't want my distorted view to ruin my marriage-to-be, so at some point I had to surrender. Surrender my anger, my negative thoughts, the way I viewed relationships with men, and the like. If this pattern is similar in nature to what you've encountered, please by all means surrender now to lighten the heartaches ahead. God can restore your view no matter what you saw at home, or needed to see at home.

When your daddy isn't there, what do you do? You tend to not know what type of relationship is right for you with a man. Oh, boy, do you learn what isn't right through trial and error. If you're fortunate enough to make the connection and become a saved believer early on, you will soon realize that men are destined to disappoint you. That said, *Proverbs 3:4-5* tells us to put our faith in God and trust Him because He is our ultimate father. For those of you who are fortunate to have an exceptional father, know that you are blessed, even those of you who are afforded the blessing of stepfathers who have come to fill in the gap or uncles who have adopted nieces to guide and provide a foundation for. You are all equally blessed. Those of us who didn't have ideal fathers to do all of the aforementioned things hoped for the blessing. Either way, I encourage you to get to know your heavenly Father.

      In the past, I'd often leave one relationship for another relationship, until I realized the relationships were all the same. Until *I* changed how I viewed relationships with men, they were all the same. Stop and think about what you've experienced, what you remember, what you saw, and everything that didn't make sense. Take a moment to remember, but don't remember all the negative things unless you're ready to release all the pain your father caused and the disappointing relationships in life. Now focus on what makes sense to you with your father. I had to tell myself, "You need love." We all do and to say you don't because you're afraid you'll be hurt the way your father hurt you isn't going to help. Remember, but forgive and release also. Surrender and forgive so you can move on with your life, since we know that Jesus died for our abundance (*John 10:10*). Forgiving is for you, not the other person.

At the end of the long road I spiraled down, I came to Front Street. I call it Front Street because it made me confront myself and ask why I would not let any man close enough to truly love me. The next thing I did was ask myself this question: Am I getting better or bitter because of baggage from past relationships, including my estranged relationship with my father? All those ugly conversations with him and the replays of the breaking furniture came immediately to mind. I had allowed myself to remain a victim of someone else's misery. I stayed in captivity, voluntarily in bondage, based on past views, thoughts, and the life I saw at home with my parents, not to mention the need I felt for a healthy relationship with my father.

Do I look like someone you know? I'm pretty sure I do. I hope that me sharing this experience will enlighten you enough to confront the struggles you might still face as a result of your relationship especially if toxic with your father. I had to determine for myself whether to discard wrongs in the past or to confront the truth. Each family member was drastically affected because of the head of household—the father.

Unfortunately, many households are affected in the same way. According to "Custodial Mothers and Fathers and Their Child Support: 2007," a report released by the U.S. Census Bureau in November of 2009, there are approximately 13.7 million single parents in the United States today, and those parents are responsible for raising 21.8 million children (approximately 26% of children under 21 in the U.S. today).

My belief, now that I know God, is that no one is fatherless. Let's be real in saying that there are many children who are fatherless in society based on single parent statistics. They are never afforded the luxury of a daddy at home with mommy to fix their bicycle, meet the school bus, come to the school for exciting programs, and the like. They *appear* fatherless, but I beg to differ. When they meet God the Father, they'll look at things quite differently. God said he'd never leave us or forsake us (*Hebrews 13:5-6*).

As a daughter, what did you see growing up and what do you see now in terms of your relationship with dad? What I truly see in my father(s) has been riveting, life changing, and worth sharing so others can learn, live, and hopefully heal from my family's experiences. The saddest thing we all discovered while sharing collectively was the disappointments and that there's still room for healing. Until recently, my father never acknowledged any wrongdoings. That's sad because some of us needed his acknowledgement early on for closure and healing, but my belief is that my father was in a place of denial or simply could not cope himself with his own plights of being a fatherless child. Believe it or not, my hope for him is that this experience will be what it is for many of you: the truth and the light in dark places so that change is inevitable.

It's amazing that even now as I think about my father the first thing that comes to mind is the many struggles for acceptance I had growing up. Have you too struggled to find acceptance from people, or just your dad, only to find acceptance does not live within the person you seek it from? We should be affirmed, accepted, and nurtured from the start but sometimes this never takes place. If this is the case for you, seek help in the one place it exists: with God. I can't stress enough that men are imperfect beings and, while we wanted and especially needed help from our flesh-and-blood fathers, we rarely if ever got it. They are designed by default to disappoint us. The magnitude of the disappointment is what makes the resounding difference.

But when I think about my heavenly father and his countless blessings, He continues to rescue me from rejection and shields me on many counts. I know just how important God's love is and to hear from him on every aspect of my life. I'd like to think that I'm a kept woman, but not in terms of how society views this phrase. I say I'm kept because God keeps me. When I don't know who, when, what, or how, He miraculously works out all details of my life. When I doubt, God reassures me that he is here and his Word is true. He will never leave or forsake you. God provided pure love to go beyond my dependency on my father or any man I've associated myself with that did not have my best interests at heart. Since walking with the Lord and our Father, this has become a common thought for me.

Until I became saved, I just didn't know how to take his unyielding, loving hand to hold me when the arms of another weren't able to do so!

I honestly think what you hear determines a lot of what you believe. The Word says, "We must pay more careful attention, therefore, to what we have heard, so that we do not drift away" (*Hebrews 2:1* NIV). Hearing some of the most dreadful statements during those dark years with my flesh-and-blood father led me straight into the arms of my heavenly Father but not before ending up in the wrong hands of a man. Because I've run to the arms of God, he's granted me spiritual growth and placed me where I can listen to Him and restore myself.

Let this be an aid to many who grew up in households where one or both parents were verbally abusive. When you walk in denial your pain may be the issue, but when you consult God on these matters, he hears your cries, listens to your petitions, and shows you that he is love. He shows you truth also. Be ready to confront the truth when you consult God. If the fact that you don't understand the magnitude of God's love doesn't appear real, just remember he sacrificed his son so that you could live—and actually live—to read this published experience.

Who knows, it may inspire you to confront those who hindered your life, your spirit, your internal growth, or all the above. No matter the person, mother or father, they have not been given the right to talk down to you or abuse you even if emotionally. What you hear is often times what you believe. What you believe you often act out. Believe the Word and listen to God when you find yourself in this situation. In your reading you'll soon discover that Jesus died for you!

Early childhood is crucial for development, and how your parents behaved in front of you can influence your behaviors in the future. Unfortunately, it can encourage you to repeat that same script you saw during childhood and act out unhealthy roles too throughout your adulthood.

I've learned through my collegiate studies as counseling major about early childhood, that we become adults who tend to operate under faulty perceptions we gathered of ourselves as children because of what we heard or saw throughout those critical developmental years at home. For refuge and healing, I encourage you to seek the ultimate Father to break free. Seek salvation and a relationship with the Lord and God. Surrender as I did and I assure you things will get better for you.

At this point, if you're willing, you can learn to understand your father and what he may or may not have done that you needed to have in your life during formative years and beyond. You can't change who your father is but you can choose to change how you interact with him to encourage healing on both sides. I'm not recommending you run from the situation but you do have to protect yourself from further injury. Of course, some situations are more detrimental than others and in some cases you need to seek peace as your guide or maintain a healthy distance to stay safe. Make safety your first priority and set healthy boundaries.

The testimony I'm sharing, as well as that of others in this book, is a deep effort to understand our combined experiences growing up with a fatherless father. The intent of our exposure is to help, not hinder by speaking the truth in love as best possible. Nor is it an opportunity to lash out and put him in a coffin with words.

As with anything in life, there's a process, just as it was a process for me to understand my heavenly Father and his love for me. I strongly urge you seek this love too. Get to know and understand your father if possible but, more importantly, take time to understand your heavenly Father. You will soon realize the differences between these fathers, along with the strong similarities. Truth be told, no one can be compared to our heavenly Father but I tend to think he equipped men to resemble him in terms of the love of a father.

If you are reading this from a place of brokenness, God is the only way out. He will reassure you by being the Father you desire to have. I, like my other siblings, could, for just entertainment purposes, tell you all the stories of what happened to us as children and daydream about what should have happened, but we would only waste time focusing on brokenness. Instead, we have focused on our truth even though that truth is not pretty. Rather than reliving disappearing acts, focus on getting a clear understanding from your father if possible about why he elected not to be there the way you wanted and needed him to be.

This can pose a challenge, depending on how you view things with your father and how you reach out for answers. I realize some fathers are nowhere to be found or simply wish not to be bothered, but you must do what is best for your healing since this is *your* life. Sure, you can continue latching on to other relationships with hopes of healing yourself, but you will arrive at a place where co-dependency on other relationships will not be enough for you to feel comforted, loved, supported, or confident in who you are as a person.

When you make this discovery, I propose a challenge: get to know our heavenly Father, God. Let's be clear, I'm not challenging you to isolate yourself from those around you who *do* support you, love you, honor you, and celebrate the person you are. I'm simply challenging you to discover what may not have worked for you as a child growing up without the bond of a father-daughter relationship, even if it includes talking to your dad to get answers. Be prepared to face and accept the truth, and do yourself a favor by allowing healing to take place the best you know how. If this is the case, then and only then can you better appreciate, understand, evaluate, and channel your attention to those who *have* fathered you through the years: an uncle, perhaps, or a mentor, a stepfather, an older brother, or, especially, God. His love is supreme and cannot be topped. He is the healer for all, no matter what the situation.

I challenge you to find a way to mend the relationship with your father before you both leave this earth. I know the idea of coming together and collaborating with someone—who may have been the cause of many hard times, missed appointments, and let downs—is a challenge. This is the beginning of the road to forgiving him. Yes, remember we have to *forgive* him. Also, remember that man is designed to disappoint and forgiving another for transgressions is really for your growth and release, not the other person.

While forgiving does not mean forgetting, it does allow light and truth to be discussed with your dad when you have the opportunity. This discussion may give you understanding and a chance for him to explain his reasons for being absent or abusive. It's okay to let him know how this has drastically affected you. It affected your growth and even your views on life. Whatever the surrounding circumstances may have been that impacted you, tell him. Truth ushers in forgiveness, freedom, deliverance, and healing, for all involved.

It was surprising to me and maybe even to others that I only began to truthfully know my father when talking with him for this book. I am grateful for and find satisfaction in the fact that this talk has ushered in truth on both sides. Throughout this journey, I've learned who this man I've called by his name for years really is. I thought there would always be an uphill battle to form a fruitful, sustained relationship with my father, but I've realized that my views on life have changed. I've accepted my truth and the truth that he may have never been able to provide fatherhood the way I'd hoped or needed. I say that because again, he comes from a place many men come from, fatherless. This is my truth and I've come to accept it however, I won't give up on the idea that God is a healer and can heal all the fatherless men who have since fathered children. Given my confidence in Christ and my age, I've moved on at this point. Although I have faith and believe God to do the impossible, some things are the way they are for a reason. Luckily, the season of not being able to really talk to my father has come and gone. I used to think this was not possible. Believe me saying, with God all things are possible so speaking with dad is possible. In fact it has become a reality in a positive way.

    My truth is that the Bible says that no weapon formed against me shall prosper (*Isaiah 54:17*). The Word is my security wall, so I no longer allow my father the authority to use words as a force to control my thoughts or behavior. I had to learn what would help me overcome and limit my exposure to such torment and abuse in nature talks.

    The Word tells us that fathers are not to exasperate their children (*Ephesians 6:4*). For this reason, I love him like a daughter should but have learned to tread lightly when he says something distasteful. For some time I also kept a healthy distance with him because I felt spending time in his element, meant hearing angry words directed towards myself, mother and siblings. I didn't need this. You have to come up with your own way of doing things to get along with your dad while protecting yourself and not being disrespectful to him as a parent.

Limiting your interactions may be a simple thing for you. Then again, it may be a journey to put limits on your own father speaking with you. It depends on you and your situation. Consult your heavenly Father on the best way to handle your flesh-and-blood father if he sits at the root of your pain, anguish, and anger. For me, praying and disconnecting from the unhealthy chatter (*2 Timothy 2:16*) has been much better than being on the receiving end of many conversations that have left me feeling less than human.

I can only speak for myself, not for others, but having a relationship with God has given me the ability to deny my father from speaking with me in such a manner anymore. In the spiritual realm, I see this being a force Satan would use to contain me or distract me from my God-given purpose. Because of the limited relationship we had for years, this is a sad situation. I will admit it's much better now because of my approach, my being led by God and my confidence in Christ; with that I have the ability to engage in conversation with my father that is healthy in nature. Without God, I'm uncertain of my ability to do so.

I truly see this experience as a lesson learned that enables me to minister to others that were raised by an unprepared father. Once I began reading the Bible I came across a variety of scriptures that met me where I was, one being (*Hebrews 12:7-12)* "Endure hardship as discipline; God is treating you as sons. For what son is not disciplined by his father? If you are not disciplined and everyone undergoes discipline, then you are illegitimate children and not true sons."

    One other detail I could not fail to mention is that I believe the Devil will use whoever or whatever in your life to distract you from being what God has called you to be. Yes, I believe he'll use even your loved ones and the power of words to penetrate your mind to tear you down. You must determine if and when you're tired of being put down by that father who has not discovered his rightful place as a man or his true identity in Christ. You'll also have to learn how to discern just how to withstand that father with grace. It was only when I met the Son, Jesus, and the Father, God, that I began to understand who I am or, better yet, *whose* I am. I am God's daughter first.

    I can remember this being a difficult and often very overwhelming lesson to learn. Because of the blood of Jesus, there is healing for all families, even those who are hurting, and specifically those fathers who hurt even themselves for what they reenacted in their own homes because they themselves grew up without fathers in the home. It tends to be a downward spiral, an unwanted curse, when a man doesn't have a father at home and doesn't get to know his heavenly Father. Don't be surprised if you feel similar in nature, or even worse, in your own life and family. Communication is the key. Let me be the first to encourage you to communicate on the level of comfort you choose though. With God's grace, this is possible. Talking it out with those close to you or those you trust helps more than you know. Praying it out is even better. Pray with a trusted friend if you're able but, no matter what, pray for God to provide direction in your life.

I can't thank God enough for standing in the gap when my father did not know how to love us or otherwise be there for me on many occasions when I needed a father. Yes, this daughter needed her father on many occasions. More than one.

For those of you who know your father, do you ever ask yourself what you inherited from him? I notice that I share a few characteristics and attributes with my father that is actually positive. He has been a homeowner for many years and I, like him, dislike the idea of renting. He has been an entrepreneur for most of his life and has held very few W-2 positions. I know I inherited his knack for entrepreneurship because I too have managed to make it on my own in the world as an entrepreneur. I must admit, I love it. This knack inside me would never allow me to simply settle for just being an employee because of my inherited, God-given talents. Not only did I inherit this from dad, all of his children are born entrepreneurs at heart, devout travelers, and risk-takers. This we know comes from dad.

Chapter 5
Dad with "Overwhelmed"
"Not able to express love to another human being"
—Overwhelmed

My mother was born in a little town down South in the early 1950s. She was the first girl of a total of fourteen siblings. She comes from a marriage union of 50+ years. With a family-centered household, mom knew nothing other than wholesome relationships as a growing child. Her early teens were a far cry from this though as she quickly became a victim of domestic violence with her first love interest. She was verbally and physically abused and eventually found herself on the run from the man who became the father of her first child, a son. Her abuse included being beaten, held hostage in an apartment for days, stabbed in her side, and cut by a long knife two additional times on her leg and thigh.

She suffered all of this for the sake of her tormentor's professed love for her and an unhealthy relationship with a man who did not hold love in high regard as her family had. After this relationship, while working in the Northeast in the early seventies, she met, became friends with, and eventually fell in love with and married my father. "The dating relationship prior to his military stint was great," she said.

They used to take breaks together while working and the relationship grew from there. "He was very well-mannered and acted like a gentleman. He worked in the cafeteria and I worked in the office. His mother worked there also."

They dated about two years. "Shortly after we met, he enlisted in the Marines. We used to visit a lot of places like Canada and New York City. This came to an end when he enlisted at the request of his mother. He enlisted primarily because his mother wanted to send him away after getting into some minor trouble with a girl in the neighborhood." This was one of the things I inherited from him. I, too, had a little trouble as a teenager with neighborhood rivals while hanging out with the wrong crowd. Funny, but true. Is it history repeating itself or me just being a careless teenager? I'll go with the latter choice.

In addition, I also see a resemblance in how my mother dated at work; so did I once in my life. I can't say this is right or wrong as I know many couples who have met spouses at their jobs, but I don't endorse this. It's obvious that watching my mother helped me to realize how much we both give so much of ourselves to others, especially significant men in our lives, that we forget to give to ourselves. Men, when you have women who will love you under such restraints, please love them back with the same strength you receive. Trust me, it's a gift.

My father served overseas while my mother waited for him. I see again how history repeats itself, as I have entertained quite a few long distance relationships. While I was full-time college student, long distance relationships worked rather well for my lifestyle, but long term they aren't the best situation. Eventually it becomes a strain mentally, physically, financially and emotionally.

We never know our selves until we investigate ourselves and the lineage we've come from. My life history has clearly shown itself in the ways I've mimicked the same relationships my mom entertained, from the way she and my father met to another relationship she was in. Remember, children replay scripts they've receive from their parents. I could ask myself why I made some of the choices I did in relationships but then I could also ask mom. I've done it for obvious reasons, in hopes of love, but then Jesus came into my life and made it more abundant, so that waiting on a man in distance wasn't necessary! Life is too short and not guaranteed to be a box of chocolates as it is, so why stress yourself with prolonged additional headaches in the form of unworthy relationships? You can wait for disappointments or you can live now! You choose.

My mother became pregnant when my father came home from the military. Actually, the baby conceived when he came home was me! So, ladies, we have learned much here: do not do this—ever! Let's challenge ourselves to not conceive a child for a man who has not committed himself in terms of becoming your mate in marriage first! If I've learned anything this far in life, a man who isn't committed to God isn't committed to himself and ultimately has no power to commit to you. Learn from those who know.

Question: Why would my mother allow such turmoil in *her* life and home, the home she arranged for herself and her child? I keep asking myself why she put up with this nonsense. I guess that, like many, me included, she hoped things would get better. Ladies, how many of us have hung around because we thought the situation or relationship or man would change for the better? Sometimes they do change but they do in their own way, and when they see fit. Sometimes the change is only temporary, so know that if a man is already a problem before marriage; the marriage will not magically change the situation. This goes for you too, men: if she's a hell-raiser now, just having your baby and becoming your wife won't negate the hell she intends to raise in your marriage. Either way, the hell is within. The only difference after that marriage is the baby and the last name. It is an inward change as a result of salvation—the Holy Ghost and the baptism of the Holy Spirit— that brings about change. Otherwise we are living in a human body operating on our own strength. I imagine this is one of many reasons why so many fatherless children exist, why single parent households are on the rise, and why so many daughters see what I have seen. Good news though: God can do what man can't. Ask, seek, and knock (*Matthew 7:7*) for His help and guided hand.

  It's one thing to have a baby outside of wedlock, but living in a common law marriage does not make the circumstances any better. Common law isn't the covenant of marriage, its just man's way of trying to implement a safety net in the absence of a covenant with God. There's no real benefit although it may feel comforting. After all, it isn't Biblical. We women are God's daughters and men are his sons. God wants abundance for us, not for our joy to be taken away by living in a situation like the one my parents lived in. My parents openly share their story not because they are ashamed but because they want me, you, and the rest of the world to learn from these mistakes. Learning here in essence may prevent a divorce in the future. Proactive is *always* better than reactive.

No one is perfect, so read this book to learn how to make your future brighter than your past. This is nonfiction and the stories are real, not misrepresentations for the purposes of entertainment. These pages reflect real lives. Perhaps my mother was more mesmerized by my father's short-lived, well-mannered approach and already in over her head with love. But, wow, did that change. Unfortunately, life decisions had already been made and she was now carrying their first child.

She regularly offered powerful quotes to her children along the path of life regarding my father: "He's incapable of loving another human being," "He's not able to show love to another human being." These are strong words to convey to your children about their father. Sadly, these words have manifested themselves in many forms throughout our lives. Fortunately for me, God the father has been that Father who with gladness took the place of what I needed, and He continues to do so daily. Without the heavenly father, this would be impossible.

Dad came into the relationship inheriting a son by my mother's previous relationship, so he instantly became a stepfather. Was he resentful? My eldest brother's actions to date represents one who appears to be a hurt child who grew up hurting those around him, including his own daughter, with verbal blows. You see readers, this stuff is for real. This is not just in the movies. The difference with the scripts in movies and the real lives presented to you here in this book is that children play the scripts of the adults at home when they too become adults. The same scripts they never intended to play get repeated, inherited by generations: cycles of scripts that have never been practiced get passed down until broken. There is power in the name of Jesus to do the very thing we need done, break the cycles!

The other sad thing is this, fathers: babies come into the world entrusted to you. What they play out in life largely depends on you as their father. The script of life you play in front of them will be replayed, believe me. What will you do from this day forward? Leave a great legacy and earn some Oscars for being Best Supporting Actor for your children. They are worth the effort. It's simplistic to state life is difficult, but allow God to help mold and shape you if you don't know how or where to begin as a great father. Repent and seek Him for salvation, so that God can become your GPS.

Remember these words I often say to you, fathers: you are the head and not the tail. Please take hold of the authority you hold in the family and make this a better society for us as a people. You hold a lot of power in what goes on at home, especially even when you are not there!

Most of the memories my mother took away from the marriage were very somber and miserable. I wonder to myself, why would she stay? In our talks she answers by saying that she prayed for God to give her the strength to endure this type of relationship so that she would have a father in the home for her children. Sadly, that is the story for many women. In the name of their children, mothers are beaten so their kids can eat; in the name of their children, women stay and die so their children can have shelter; in some cases, the mother, in the name of her children, stays for clothing, or healthcare, or material objects, but these women pay a healthy price physically, mentally, financially, and spiritually. Really in every way they pay!

Why does it have to be this way? Watch the news, read the reports in the newspapers about domestic violence, just pick a reason why women stay and more than likely they would have been covered on this aforementioned list! Know this, fathers: you control what's reported in the media, too. What will it say concerning you? Just imagine how many families don't report the things that go on in their homes. For me, this has now been close to thirty years and the memories of pain are still very present. Many times my mother didn't make the news but her pain was very real and she stayed, according to her, for her children to have a father in the home. To her I say, "Okay," but she should not have chosen this for herself. In the end, we all suffered in the meantime. She was a living sacrifice. Fathers, I respect you when you move on, but take care of your own. Trust me, I respect that. Its better when you know she isn't the one and move on, but don't move on from being that dad you know you should be to your kids. If you divorce her, please don't divorce your children.

    In the case of my mom, would you say this was dysfunctional love, low self-esteem, or her need to be loved at the cost of herself and her children? Believe it or not the more you talk to parents the more you'll hear similar statements, especially from our mothers and grandmothers who were homemakers.

    Shortly before my entrance into this world, mom worked herself to a point where she and I both almost died during childbirth. In pain, and surely emotionally distraught, mom went to the hospital alone in a taxi cab. As a result of my premature birth, she had to stay in the hospital for nine days. What a vision: a young pregnant women working until a kind co-worker calls a taxi cab, only to nearly die on the way to giving birth to a baby girl. Not exactly what you aspire to as a young lady.

    I certainly am not envisioning myself going to the hospital in a cab pregnant, alone, and nearly dying in the backseat. Come on, women, this isn't what we dream of as little girls thinking about a beautiful wedding day and having kids. It all comes back to the choices we make and they often as women start with who we choose to have in our lives. Dad and her never should have gone beyond the word, "Hello." Better stated, they only should have remained co-workers. Some relationships are better left just in passing than to take on such burdens.

However, God had a plan. I see so many things in my own life that resemble the remnants of my parent's lives. Really looking at this for what it is, I have to be careful to not repeat such tragedies or pass this on to my descendants. The common thread is the fact that they didn't have Christ involved and lacked his guiding hand. Carnal decisions lead to carnal results.

It's better to know the history of your parents and learn to pray for change so that familial "challenges" can be that of "inherited blessings" going forward from your generation. Better yet, ask God to change the patterns in your parents' generation while they are still living so that their lives will be blessed. I've learned this is vital and important so that I don't pass on dysfunctional patterns to generations to come. The devil is surely a liar on this one. God, not Satan, will get the glory because of what I've learned from the testimony of my mother and father.

Through all of my life the Heavenly Father was there, but always my flesh-and-blood father. Fathers please pay close attention to the effect this has had on our family. You have the ability to either damage your children or have a resoundingly positive effect on them. I keep asking you: what will your children say about you?

You see, fathers, a daughter needs you daily. Never let her appearance, her disposition, her independence, or even her distance tell you otherwise. You are the parent so take the initiative to water your little pumpkin's smiling face daily by keeping in touch with your daughter, and supporting her.

As my mother looks back at her situation, I remember her confessions of the relationship being doomed from the beginning because she was stable with herself and her first son. She had money saved and a good place to live, a success story for a single mother in the early seventies. Because she thought that a marriage to my father was the right thing to do for her and for her children, she paid for the marriage license herself. What a travesty from the very beginning!

Why didn't either of my parents consult God on such a major life decision? He would not have wanted this for either. Although He is a forgiving God, the decisions of my parents were not made with decency and order. Shouldn't my father have been the one seeking marriage, and the one financially preparing for his upcoming marriage, preparing for his new wife and stepson? I'd think so. Knowing him now, he'd tell me, his daughter, to expect nothing less in a man.

Unfortunately, there were many days of physical fighting and arguing while she was pregnant with one or another of my siblings. I can assure you in her actions, verbal cues and confessions she regrets the entire situation from the beginning, from the very first day my father walked into her life. In fact, based on both of their memories of life as a couple, life beyond co-workers as previously mentioned was probably not a good choice for each of them. Note to self: assess the relationship up front. If there are red flags that scream, "Stop," pay close attention.

Ask your friend, the Holy Spirit, to reveal what should be regarding the relationship. A woman once said if you even see pink signs, not fully developed as red signs don't further entertain the relationship because as you know the color pink can quickly turn to the color red which means big signs and a strong indication that the marriage may not last.

Just as with the birth of their first child together, me, their second child came into the world prematurely and with complications. Baby Number Two had to remain in the hospital for two months until being released. Could the premature births be a testament to the ungodly nature of their relationship, premature and immature as it was?

Perhaps so. The stress, the domestic violence, and the loveless relationship took their toll on my mother's physical frame and her unborn babies. Thank God for our Heavenly Father, as he carried her during birth and helped bring the babies into the world. It was God's healing and protection that did not allow Satan to take any of our lives. Praise the Lord.

A disturbing thought that has taunted me throughout life is that we kids were not allowed to call my father "Daddy." What a designed disconnect from the very beginning. What kid doesn't want to call their father "Daddy"? That word more than often comes from a sign of affection and to be told not to call him "Daddy" was hideous.

My mother, when speaking about her own father—my grandfather—acknowledged that she felt that her, her parents and thirteen siblings had a good family life coming up. She recalls them having financial hardships but living a peaceful life. Her father was very supportive, a good dad with whom she had a good relationship although he was a very hands off father. She was born in a house by midwife in the Deep South. There were also other siblings born by midwife in their home my grandfather built with his hands with three of my uncles. Can you imagine being born in a house by midwife? Unbelievable! In the fifties this was common. Thank God for advanced medical care and technology.

Her story and the story of her fiancé at the time—my eldest brother's father—is one we've all heard of at least once in our lives. If we haven't heard it in real life, we've seen on the movie screen. Sadly, some young ladies are drawn away by the wrong men. My mother ran away with my eldest brother's father only to find out that he would get her pregnant, beat her, nearly kill her twice, and attempt to practice bigamy with her since she later discovered that he was already married to another woman. What a devastating situation to survive. Thankfully, she did survive. She was able to get away from him but not before he came back a final time to make an attempt to kidnap their son and attempt to murder her when she tried to stop him. Needless to say he was very, very abusive.

Because of the Eternal Father again, the Father to the fatherless regardless of the situation, she lived to tell the story. Little did she know when they met on a double date that this man would be the one she would have to flee because of his violent temper and repeated abusive acts.

All the signs point to her perception of the ideal father not being mature in the ways she needed. Why else would she have remained in these abusive relationships? Did she know God? She grew up as a Baptist and in early adulthood converted to a Seventh Day Adventist. When the mood of my conversation with my mother lightens, she even speaks of the two evangelists, Oliver Johnson and his wife, who gave their witness to her and led her to convert to a Seventh Day Adventist many years ago.

Because of Mr. Johnson and his wife, she's been walking with the Lord for quite some time now. Was she not aware she could transform her world, as *Romans 12:2* says, and renew her mind? I'd have to say she experienced a learning curve until salvation could truthfully set in. For her it was unfortunate that she had to experience so much mistrust, damage, and abuse before salvation. Otherwise, the ending to the movie of her life during those abusive years might look different. Some say your mess is your message and in this case her experiences would eventually be her message to share with her children. I say that because we children could see her being hurt; the painful statements and the bitter conversations regarding the entire situation said so. When all is said and done, though, thankfully she persevered beyond both the failed relationships.

It's better for us as parents to share our experiences with our children so that they too can learn from our lives prior to becoming parents themselves. The understanding that the Heavenly Father can help lead and guide you is very important for them to know and learn early in life. God can lead and guide you in terms of talking with your children about life experiences that may affect their future. While it may not be apparent at the time that your message is having an effect on them, please realize it has a lasting effect. For me I had a distorted image of my father because my mother vented to us openly and described him in an unhealthy way at home. Then, when spending time with him, I struggled with acceptance because of the distorted view that had been portrayed about him, the person she'd been describing all year long. Sometimes this left me feeling confused. Words have life and many of her words came to life concerning the man she often described. Sadly, some was truth as we know it.

I do believe our testimony is the beginning of a great ministry to help others in similar situations. By running from your purpose and not spending time with

God will prevent you from understanding this. However, my parent's testimony is powerful in that those reading can learn valuable lessons. Both ladies and men can learn from such devastation that they should avoid such dysfunctional relationships. God is good though, as he has restored her life beyond one bad marriage and an even worse engagement.

Parents, there's a never a good time for you to blast the other parent in their absence, particularly in front of your kids. Trust me on this one. Save the blasting for private conversations with other adults in pure confidence only. Please, read this with clarity and take it from someone who knows. My hope is that you remain positive with your daughter. I say this because, as a mother, you don't want your daughters growing with a distorted view of men. Likewise fathers, you don't want your daughters growing up with a distorted view of you or what other men look like if you have not been there. Either way, the damage will be detrimental.

Fathers, you want your daughters, as growing ladies, to see you as the most important man in her life so that she can build strong relationships with other men. She will especially need a strong relationship with the man who will become her husband one day.

Fathers, share your life stories with your daughter so that she will understand you for the man you were even prior to becoming her father. Believe it or not, history is important. Fathers, your history with your daughter could be very instrumental in allowing her to form better opinions of what type of man she should date. Of course the goal of dating is marriage, so your impressions give her insight on who she should be courted by or even marry.

Mothers, talking bad to your little girls could cause you to make your girls never have hope that a man can treat her right or love her because they are *all* no good. You plant the seed for little pumpkin to grow up thinking they're all liars and that no one will ever measure up. This is not true. There is someone who will love them unconditionally in this world. Think on that and share that before you blast negativity, which can only lead to distrust later in life and potentially leave your daughter alone! Parents, is this what you want for your daughters?

Mothers, I know—as a mother myself—that this isn't what you want for your little girls. You want little princess happy and prosperous. Fathers, daddy's little girl is leaving home one day, so why not have her blessed in spirit, with a positive outlook regarding her prince charming on the way. Your interactions—the words you speak about that other parent—all have a lasting effect. Believe me. It's too costly to breed negativity. Your mission is to breed the opposite: positivity.

My mother felt strongly that my father was angry at his own mother most of the time and even perhaps her too and lashed out at anyone who would listen. Since, as his wife, she was the closest person to him, she would be the one who would listen to the emotional abuse during their thirteen years together.

Later, after their divorce, that person became me, who without consent was forced to listen in on too many ill-willed conversations. I took my mother's place and became the one who listened to him and all of his let-downs even if I only called just to say hello. Many of those conversations became frustrating sessions for me that became harder to bear. Besides that, I was not the root of the wrong decisions and poor choices made.

Fathers, please understand that your children are not your therapists and don't need to have you dump your problems in their laps about your former wife, which is likely their mother. It's different if these are your adult children but as young minors, teenagers and adolescents, I beg you not to use your conversations with your kids as therapy.

Fathers, I can't say it enough: what your children need and deserve is your undivided attention, your love, your help, your protection, and your support. They really need to be led by example, to be led to Christ and everything else that nurtures healthy and balanced people. Anything else is clearly setting them up to fail in life.

I'm a firm believer that you have many choices in life. I've lived long enough to see the difference in my life after I surrendered my plans for God's plans & my will for God's will. Trust me; the latter is better than the former. I have since adopted the motto of "Him first, me second." That is God's will, mines is secondary. Certainly this is the case in my personal relationships.

Surrender to God if you don't know how to be a good man, fiancé, husband, or father. God is here to help you all the way through. Have you ever considered giving yourself away to your Heavenly Father? Try it and you just might be relieved and, better yet, surprised by the relief of your burden.

Mothers' actions say that she loved my father more than herself. This was an unfortunate thing considering the mental anguish in this relationship. From the affair to the dysfunctional and abusive relationship they had kept her disappointed but not enough to leave sooner. When people say that, "I stayed for my children," what does that do to them as a person? I'll tell you based on what this daughter has seen: it can appear to make you bitter and hopeless about ever being worthy to receive the love you're worth. It also makes your self-esteem spiral out of control. Staying in an unhealthy and dysfunctional relationship damages you more than it helps you in the long run.

One of the most detrimental things when you commit infidelity is what it does to the people who were not even a part of the actual act: your family. Fathers, being in the home destroying the wife while your children are watching are true acts of travesty and sincerely unhealthy. Leaving isn't always the worst idea when such turmoil and dysfunctional behavior takes over your home. Preserve your children's inherent positive outlook as best you can. Again fathers, please be the head and not the tail. Spend time with God, following his examples as a man of the Word.

It was a big deal when my mother told my father that she was expecting their first child. Now, men, women really are sensitive about how you'll handle this news. I realize this is life-changing, so be sensitive with your response. Be careful about your reaction when a woman tells you that she is expecting your child. My prayer is that you'll consider the feelings of all parties involved, and not just your own feelings.

My mother recalled how she shares life changing news of their expected child. She says that moment spoke volumes and set precedence for what was to come in their future. It was evident they both were not happy. Apparently this is an issue for many unplanned pregnancies, the couple being unpleasantly surprised that a baby is soon to come. Talk about another disconnection early in my life.

Ladies, when is enough, enough? Men, when is enough, enough? Should you be real before the marriage even begins when you sense and see the looming heartache ahead? On many days, we as their children felt the heavy weight of depression mixed with verbal abuse and sometimes physical abuse that was heavy enough to make me the average person take their own self out. Her prayer was that God would allow her to see her children become adults. He honored her prayer, thankfully.

Her testimony up to this point could never have prepared me for what we learned about the hinging affair in their marriage: the act of infidelity took place in our home and in my parents' bed. How can people be so insensitive to one another? My idea is that when a person loves another the way God intended they consider the other person over themselves before acting.

The Bible makes it clear, in *Ephesians 5*, how a man should love his wife and a wife loves her husband. Obviously this marriage was not being guided by the Father from inception. This says to me, their daughter, that this story could have been different provided our Heavenly Father was apart of the union. I'm not afraid to admit, some relationships are not meant to go beyond, "Hello." Some relationships are only meant to be friendships and so often we mess this up by stretching them beyond their season or reason.

Some may argue that infidelity actually can be overcome but when you already have so many other uphill challenges, some marriages may not make it. I, too, even though not married, can see this as a deal-breaker in a marriage. God does not like divorce, but it is pardoned for infidelity (see *Matthew 19:3*). Not that I advocate for divorce but trust and insecurities became the focus, never mind the betrayal and deception and the child outside of the marriage. The Bible tells us "with God all things are possible" (*Matthew 19:26*) but have you considered the idea that God was not a part of this union? As time would ware on, surely, my mother's prayer was to seek God for help out this catastrophe.

The affair created a discourse for those who suffered the consequences, the children. In return the divorce was inspired. As a fractured family we would soon relocate to another city in an attempt of reconciliation, although it failed. In the interim, the children were without grandparents support, aunts, uncles' etc. because we moved down south to the infamous Gate Way Village Apartments. At the time, moving to a new location for a fresh start if they were going to rebuild their union was the idea that prompted the decision. Primarily, the move was to get away from the adulterous affair. The move gave hope that the infidelity would stop but it never did. The sad part is that even though we moved away, the damage was apparent and dad still was not often home with his family. We left the comforts of our home and the support of a large extended family for nothing.

Living proof of this fact showed itself for the rest of their time together as a couple. Like many affairs, it produced a child outside of wedlock. This was the straw that broke the camel's back. It was then a done deal: the child conceived would end the marriage. The marriage officially was over.

What remained; 6 individuals, broken pieces and heartache filled memories that still have the ability to hurt and haunt us all. Otherwise, as all of us children have stated, it was in vain. For me, things got worse. I was very young and wished we could have remained near the support of our extended family instead of moving away from those aunts, uncles, cousins, and grandmothers that I needed in my life. So you see, the man of the house is important; he is *vital*. Many decisions are made as a result of his involvement, whether good or bad. Fathers, what decisions are being made as a result of your involvement?

Our house in the Northeast, although beautiful on the outside was still not a home. It was an empty dwelling where a woman and four children cared for themselves while the husband and father left them for other things—more important things, so he thought—in the streets. Fathers, do you see yourself in this scenario, or at least responsible for leaving your family at home for other things of interest in the streets? This is simply a question to prompt some reflection.

Ladies, we stay. Although for different reasons, even when we know that our significant other isn't who God called us to be with. Why did she stay? Oh, I remember: for us kids. If I were old enough then I would have said, "leave!"

What's so sad is the discovery of the affair and the confession of the other woman. Of course guys if you leave this up to two women to discuss, more details will be forth coming opposed to being straight with your partner, spouse and wife. When women discuss the details they include it all and due to hurt feelings may not leave a single shred of details out regarding your involvement. The best case scenario; be true to your self and move on if the marriage is no longer what you desire. The alternative looks very similar to the story you're reading. Talk about deception. The funny thing is that I remember some parts of what has been described as if yesterday.

Fathers, how can you think your children would not comprehend such things? Children are very observant and when we don't think they understand, they surprise us. Men, don't do this to your children. This is a sign of disrespect to your family. Better yet, it's a sign of disrespect to you. Why take vows if you're not going to take them seriously?

Fathers, the lesson in this is situation is to simply love your wives as clearly as it states in the Bible. If so, you won't have to experience this situation in your own marriage if you follow the plan for our lives. Yes we are human but we have to remember why we picked that wife. Yes, temptation is real but it has a cost that you don't see when you're in that moment of lust with that person who is not your spouse. There is no reward for affairs, none. In the end two shattered families were affected the existing and the newly created one because another woman and child too suffered. No one won in the end. Just think about it.

Mothers and wives, you too have valuable lessons to learn here. The mistress obviously had a need that needed to be met since she was estranged from her husband. This projected her need to be captured by another man since her's was incarcerated. Can we as women do more at home to capture and keep the apple of our husband's eye or would you say regardless of what you do, a roaming eye will roam? Ladies, can we do more to inspire them to not cheat or have roaming eyes?

Mothers, even if married with four children, our men need love too. To survive infidelity is hard. Once we moved apart into a single family home, I rarely recalled mom crying in front of us. As I think back, she likely fought hard to hold it together enough to speak kind words about him. I see her method of coping with the pain by the venting and by being very frank with us about her despising this man. At any rate, truth be told, she is still so very strong to have endured years of torment from love interest in her past and even so the man she said "I do" to in marriage.

Parents let me say again that your children aren't an audience for negative language about the other parent; however, some of you will be better than others in terms of hiding your pain. Naturally you will operate within your level of comfort, but my prayer is that you take confessions, resentment, anger, and venting about your disgusts and disappointments to God and not your children.

My dream used to be that my parents could at least be civil or even friends, for the sake of their children whom have since reached adulthood. However, I have to admit, I never walked their shoes in this marriage the way she did and can't judge or force my opinion on the matter. Each person's experience is different and needs to be respected. I wouldn't be surprised if healing has not taken place for my mother. You can forgive but the pain reminds you not to forget so that you don't allow such a scenario to manifest itself again.

After all of that pain, my mother owed it to herself to love better and be loved by better. These commentaries come straight from the heart. They are not fabricated and these are not actors, these were real life recounts of what I saw. These are people who played a role they never auditioned for, prepared for, or sought out. These were our lives. Note that I said "*were* our lives."

My mom should have questioned a lot more within herself, followed her intuitive inner voice inside and definitely consulted God on the matter to spare herself as a vessel of pain. In sharing with me, she admits she definitely should have left sooner than eleven years after they first met. Ladies I'd caution and say the qualities we desire in a man are all cute, tall, slender, bald, black, white, etc. but what about the fruit of the spirit which are love, peace, joy, kindness, self-control, patience, faithfulness, gentleness and goodness. This depiction shows no signs of having the fruit of The Spirit whatsoever.

You see, men, you can know that you have that good thing from God—see *Proverbs 18:22*—and still not know how to cherish it. Why mess with God's daughter? I can see on the other side how a man would take advantage of this woman who only wanted change within the house and apparently love at "all cost".

Ladies, we must know our worth. See *Proverbs 31* for some insight. *Matthew 7:6* reads, "Don't not throw your pearls to pigs." Sounds pretty harsh, but the Bible does not lie. When we are upside down in relationships, like pigs the other person takes, never giving or replenishing. The pig is only there to take, especially if you allow it to take from you. Evaluate what type of relationship you have. Is it giving to you or taking from you?

Mom recalls how she aspired to be a nurse and studied at a local Technical College, even though she never had support from her union or agreed help with the care of the children, let alone emotional or financial support. For that reason, she settled for a shorter program in Secretarial Science, resulting in jobs she truly did not care for. She settled in love, marriage, career and her education which in turn made her settle in life. Why did she make such choices? My guess is her own father didn't enlighten her, but her Heavenly Father since has. Life has drastically improved for her ever since.

My question is: Where were her parents in all of this, in particularly her own father? Oh, I can tell you: not consumed with his daughter's life. Although granddad was very nice, God rest his soul, he took a very passive role in his daughter's life. He was not assertive in suggesting anything better for her and acted as if he was eating a box of popcorn while watching a bad movie. This is the choice you have as passive fathers: you can watch devastation or you can take the leading role in the life of your "little precious" and help her to become all that she has been called to be. Passivity doesn't work.

I'm glad my mother went back to high school after dropping out and on to college because I, having walked some of the same footsteps in relationships, admire her determination and strength to make it through sour experiences with little support, help, and love from her own father.

Her determination makes her a hero to me, her only daughter. I still admire her strength. For many years we wondered why she wouldn't remarry or entertain relationships, but now I understand why. She needed healing, peace, and love. Sometimes the Heavenly Father is the only one who can do that for a season.

I don't, however, support her choice to sacrifice herself and stay in a toxic marriage. But I do understand why her thinking would allow her to do so at that time. I believe she felt unworthy of loving herself more than the man in her life. She allowed my father to play on her low self-esteem. She allowed Satan to penetrate her thoughts and convince her that she needed my father more than living without him and all that heartache and pain for so long. Neither her fiancé nor her husband ever should have been marriage choices and neither of them matched her involvement in the relationship. At best, maybe they could have had a friendship, but nothing beyond that. Evaluate yourselves. Do you see any resemblances? What do you see?

I can't say I would have done the same but her testimony is my lesson to really examine the fruits of the behavior concerning the man to whom I will say "I do." After all, the marriage will be a covenant between me, him, and God and in my eyes that makes it worthy of profound examination.

As my mother and I continue to talk I hear remnants of disappointment, some un-forgiveness, and definitely some bitterness. Can you blame her, though? I certainly don't blame her but can appreciate her need for forgiveness in spite of the choice to marry, have children and stay with my father for such a time. Again, at best I see my father only having been in a position to be a friend, and that only maybe.

Fathers, you are the first to know whether or not you're capable of being a spouse or a father. Be honest to the women you are with and make sound decisions early not to entrap, feed false hope, or mislead. Committing to a relationship and having children are life changing decisions. They have a lasting effect on those who come from your union: the children. Even just having a casual even if consensual sexual relationship outside of marriage comes with a responsibility; that's why God only intended sex for married couples.

Based on what you've read so far, surely you must agree sex is worth preserving until marriage so God can bless your union. The best benefit for a marriage I see is salvation for each individual first. Coming to know Christ for yourself is a gift from God and sets things in order prior to any relationship leading up to marriage.

Overall, my mother tried to carry the weight of all of this—the marriage, the infidelity, the children—on her shoulders, only for her to be overwhelmed and need to retreat into divorce. Her legacy says a lot. She is a survivor; she is her children's hero even though we had no idea of her sacrifice at the time. When I ask her how this makes her feel, she says, "Hmmm, I wasn't mad at first, but it hurt me."

Truthfully, the only way I see her fully recovered from the many disappointments—like going to the hospital in a cab by herself to deliver her baby, or discovering her husband and mistress in her bed in her home—is through her knowing her Heavenly Father, God. What she faced as a result of just going past the word "Hello" with my father was not worth all she endured. Yes, I do realize her not going beyond "Hello" means I might not be in this world. I love her enough to say that that would have been fine, if it meant she didn't have to live at my father's heel for so many years.

As she thinks back on her life prior to her union with him she recalls always having money when it was just her and her first son. "I would travel with him and go back and forth to New York often." For them as she recounts without my father, life was good.

Chapter 6
Dad with "Homeless and Searching"

"Every daughter wants to hear her daddy say it's going to be alright."
—Homeless

Sonya*:* Where does the title originate from?
Homeless and Searching*:* The title comes from my perception as a daughter based on a relationship I have with my birth father, and a relationship I've come to have with my Heavenly Father. As a child, I always had this perception of what my family should be compared to how my family actually was. A couple of years ago, my flesh-and-blood father made what I thought was an insulting statement about a business plan that I wanted to share with him.

He kept telling me, "You need to write a book, you need to write a book." I didn't want to be an author. I never realized that skill was in me. I'm not creative like that and didn't think I was creative enough to follow through with such a task. But when you allow God to birth in you purpose, all things are possible. The key is being open to birthing the vision given to you by God.

That said, the title came clear to me one day soon after an insulting statement from my father in 2007. I always lived with the need to gain acceptance from my father and simply wanted to get the blessing from him on a business plan and in some areas of my life. Little did I know—though surely God did—this book was going to come forward and be birthed as a result of my flesh-and-blood father's many unwanted words. You could say that he motivated me to get to the point of writing. He began some time ago stating that I was to write a book about him even though I had aspired not to do such a thing. Surprisingly it's about him but profoundly and really sadly displays the hurt his immediate family encountered. It's surely not something he intended.

Sonya: So the book is about two relationships, with your birth father and the Heavenly Father, your perception of what your family is versus to what you thought it should look like. You also said that he spoke the book into existence.

Homeless and Searching: Yes, by stating I should write years ago.

Sonya: What does your family look like?

Homeless and Searching: As a child, we watched *The Cosby Show* and that's what I thought a family should look like: two loving parents in the home. The family is the first institution that a child comes to know. So for me, watching the Cosby's and knowing other children that I befriended and seeing their parents gave me an indication that my family was odd. I was always aware that my picture of what a family should look like was the total opposite of what we had. It was always in my head that this isn't the picture of an ideal family but I also realized that the Cosby show isn't real life either. It was a dream to have a regular family and ever since then I've kept the hope of having a family alive.

My father was in the home until I was eight years old. Prior to him leaving, he was there but it wasn't a strong family unit. There was a lot of domestic violence. We had times when we did things as a family but it didn't outweigh the other times. In fact, the majority of the time we did not do things together as a family.

Sonya: You had mentioned the mental abuse and how you didn't' know that's what it was. What's your first recollection of domestic violence and the mental abuse?

Homeless and Searching: My first recollection of domestic violence is… the day my parents had a public fight in front of the community at Gateway Village in the eighties. I will never forget that. To see them fighting at home was one thing but to see them in public was my first vivid memory of domestic violence. That was the first day of major separation in the family because once that fight happened we never went back to a family unit. That was the end of that. As I look at it all, we were not very much of a family prior to that either.

Sonya: So your father never came back into the home?

Homeless and Searching: No. He never came back. From there I, my mother, and my other siblings went to a shelter. That was truly the beginning of our separation. That particular fight, even though there were others, was the end. After that my mother went into seclusion and had limited to no contact with my father.

***Sonya*:** Did all of your brothers also witness the public violence?
***Homeless and Searching*:** Yes. From then on, I became the communicator for the family because my mother would no longer speak to my father. So the mental abuse would come by way of him: "Your mother is this, your mother is that." He would put my mom down. He'd want me to go into a place of denial with him. He'd say, "I never hit your mother." I would always hang up the phone when I had to communicate for the both of my parents, feeling rejected and worse. Or I'd feel ashamed to have to be in a situation where I had to call him and ask for money, or ask for anything for that matter. Even though I was only asking for essential needs for his children, he made me feel awful asking him for anything. I'd tell the fathers out there, please think twice so your little girl feels safe to come to her dad for help. Don't let your little precious go through feeling she can't ask dad for anything. Please! Otherwise she may be in the vulnerable position of having to ask others.

    I remember having to build myself up to ask him for bare essentials for my brothers and me. I mean simple things like food to eat, electricity, or perhaps school supplies. Asking made me have to grit my teeth and feel queasy. The pain of the words he would say back to me was often times unbearable. Often the words slashed my little ego and self-esteem to the ground, just asking for money from a father who lived like a king.

For this reason, in times past I tried very hard to avoid contact with him until I had healed. Because of the Lord, I had to pursue healing from years of a devastating and non-supportive relationship with my father.

Sonya: I want to come back to the incident where you saw fighting.

Homeless and Searching: I saw my parents fighting often. Each time they did we saw them fighting because it was in front of us.

Sonya: What were you feeling?

Homeless and Searching: I felt sadness, fear, and disconnection. A lot of times I cried because it hurt so much to see my parents fighting and using language to tear one another apart. I hated it. I'd tell men and women to shield and shelter their children from their fighting so they can protect their children from feeling this type of way. It's no benefit to see this behavior. Trust me; it leaves a lasting impression on your children's hearts, minds and even their development as a person. It takes a lot of effort to get past seeing this domestic violence and you have to want hard to get beyond the brokenness it causes. Please, parents, consider your children.

Sonya: What were you thinking?

Homeless and Searching: I was thinking to myself, "God, why is this happening?" What did we do to have parents tear each other apart this way? I was just a child and at that time can honestly remember asking, "Why God? Why?"

I remember staring and crying during the last big fight at Gateway. It was out in the street for everyone to see, all the neighbors, our friends. It was like watching a terrible fight in the streets when it happened and I remember running and crying. Come to think about it, I grew up accustomed to do a lot of that! I run and cry. I run from relationships out of fear and in the way, I cry. I cry because I hate the end result but it often times seems easier to end it than to endure any pain as a result of a lifetime of brokenness. On the flip side, I've learned that running and crying were not meant to be lifetime commitments. I see now that God is clearly not one to have his daughter running and crying. So I don't cry anymore and I no longer fear, but more importantly I no longer run. I seek Him and ponder ideas, dreams, hopes and desires. I have surrendered to Him, so the running has stopped. Now I stand. I stand on the Word of God.

Sonya: Then you went to a shelter and your mom put you in the middle.

Homeless and Searching: I was their oldest child. Looking back I understand why she did it. I don't think she realized my ears would replace hers, though. If she had, maybe something else would have taken place for her to shield me.

Sonya: Your father belittled you.

Homeless and Searching*:* I remember being asked which parent I wanted to live with. My mom used me as a communicator because she couldn't do it anymore. I understand why now. She needed to give herself a break from the nonsense conversations, but I guess she didn't realize the magnitude of unhealthy exposure I'd be subjected to for being the communicator between my parents.

Sonya: Did dad ever say other hurtful things to you as a child?

Homeless and Searching: Yes. When I was a child he mentioned this awful noise I made as a result of having allergies. He would say, "You're never going to get a man doing that." He would say that to me as a result of something as simple as clearing my throat from having allergic reactions. Evidently, I had issues with hay fever and my sinuses. He could have concerned himself with why I made the noise, like the health reason behind the noise. Is wanting love and support asking too much from a father? But the most hurtful thing was the business plan I shared with him. I also feel like I've been doctoring many verbal wounds for many years. Speaking to him often takes me back to uncovering the wound and pouring salt right on top of it. I was coming to him for emotional support, not financial support.

Sonya: So really your whole life you've been looking for acceptance.

Homeless and Searching: Pretty much as a result of the weak relationship with him I've been searching for love and have felt homeless my whole life. Recently, though, I started feeling very disconnected and as if I no longer need his acceptance. If it has to come through the form of verbal abuse, I'll pass. I no longer desire or pursue his acceptance, because my faith with the Lord has given me balance and I feel God's love. That's why I don't share with him much about me anymore; I don't tell him any of my plans, only the basics. Because I've defaulted to thinking he doesn't care anyway. To him it seems as if what I'm sharing really doesn't matter. He's shown his children that.

Sonya: So you took a chance to share your business and he said, "You're never going to make it, it's not going to happen." So your take is that's the last time you'll share anything significant.

Homeless and Searching: Yes. We went a year without real communication because I was worn out with such negative input, no support from him, and a lack of anything worth holding on to. At the end of the day I still needed my father, and I realize I need my Heavenly Father as my dad.

Sonya: How did that feel?

Homeless and Searching: Peaceful, honestly. I didn't hear any abuse, any rejection, any insults or anything that would further injure my delicate soul. That year felt like a year of growth for me. During that time I declared to myself—which was really unfortunate—that if I left this earth prematurely before speaking with my father again, that was a decision I would be alright with. I also determined out of frustration and pain in the same thought, that if he passed before we were ever able to speak again, that would be alright, too. I took my silence as a sign of needing to heal and grow in the direction to love myself more, rather than subject myself to negativity by allowing him to continue to dump on me. I want to live in abundance and I was willing to take that chance for many years. I didn't miss the ugly conversations with him. Some might say this is sad, but I say it's simply the truth.

He's always downed my mom. He'd say some nice things but they don't outweigh the bad things he said. It's almost like, when hearing him say nice things, it doesn't even matter. They seem artificial because the bad things he's said about my mom or any of us in the family has had such a lasting impression on me. I'd share with the fathers out there that how you portray your little girl's mother may just determine how she portrays her own self-worth. I struggled over the years when men would give me compliments—my dad's voice always seems to overshadow the good things being shared with me. What I mean is that I can't take a compliment for fear of having the compliment overshadowed by the bad comments made about me soon thereafter. Or the other thing is that I will second guess the sincerity of the man complimenting me at the time. Screwed up, I know. I've had to come a long way with understanding that all men are not here to harm. In fact, many have been kind to me and very sincere in spite of how I looked at myself, whether good or bad.

I came to realize that my father wanted us to live in denial about him verbally, psychologically, and physically abusing our mom. Truth be told, he wanted us to live in denial about verbally abusing us, too.

Sonya: Has your father ever taken responsibility for his actions against your mom?

Homeless and Searching*:* I asked him whose fault it was that the marriage didn't work. He said it was his fault during my interview with him. Other than admitting the failed marriage, he's never admitted anything about verbally abusing his children. In fact, he'll be quite surprised by all our confessions here. Lately, I see at times his efforts to reestablish and build workable relationships with us. Sometimes we just don't care enough to re-establish back, though. We are all tired of the verbal blows. Although we're tired of it, we are grateful for the turn of events in the nature of our relationship with him. At the end of the day, we are family and need healthy relationships with each other. Surprisingly dad will at times say things like, "I was the best father," which is a boldfaced lie. I'd disagree, and my brothers would, too. He has never admitted that he was not the best father or a bad husband.

***Sonya*:** So what's your perspective on your childhood as your father's daughter?

Homeless and Searching: My birth father or my Heavenly Father?

***Sonya*:** Your birth father.

***Homeless and Searching*:** I don't feel like my birth father was ever really there for me as a child. I never felt his true protection as a little girl. Many days, in fact, I felt as if I were a patient in the hospital wearing a gown that exposed my rear end. I always felt uncovered and in search of cover. Shamefully, I feel as if I often looked and desired for a father figure in men that I've dated in the past. I've come to understand my need to have that protection especially that covered feeling that comes out of being rejected and denied as a little girl for so long. It wasn't until I developed a relationship with my Heavenly Father that I realized I am covered, I am protected, and especially that I am taken care of and I'm no longer homeless and in search of the greatest love. I realized this, but not before many days filled with emptiness. God has shown me on more than one occasion that his unchanging hand is here. It always was and always will be. God never leaves us.

Sonya: Compare and contrast your relationship between your father and God.

Homeless and Searching: With my flesh-and-blood father, I felt maybe like I was his niece but never a daughter. With God, I feel and know I'm covered like a daughter should be. God accepts me for me. He was there for my conception, birth, and every aspect of my life when I often didn't act like a daughter who deserved His love or even God's mercy, favor, and grace.

My father didn't give unconditional love, but God did. I kept trying to give unconditional love to my father but kept getting rejected no matter how hard I tried. I look back and wonder why I was trying so hard to love and gain acceptance from someone who really didn't care enough to grant me that. He would tell you differently but for someone who never showed you love, how would you know or believe that they love you? Fathers, take the time to show your daughters that you really love them. Invest in their lives, their interests, their goals, their ambitions—everything that matters—so they will be affirmed by you and not some man in the street. Don't take this chance, because it's costly. We tend to find love in the worst places as wounded people. I'm not saying there aren't diamonds in the rough but there's a faith walk when taking this approach.

God is going to take care of his children no matter what. He has shown me that he will take care of me, his daughter. Once, when I was terribly sick, I could have been called home in that hospital bed but God spared my life. God didn't take my life and like a loving Father he healed me. He healed me from many relationships in the past and can heal you, too. I've come a long way and still have a ways to go but will get better as I focus on my Heavenly Father more.

Remember, God has been there for all things in my life: my birth, my high school graduation, my college years as a struggling student, my first home, businesses, business plans, first office, relocations, and a failed engagement, along with other failed relationships. My flesh-and-blood father was there for none of these things.

Sonya: Has he ever mentioned that he loved you?
***Homeless and* Searching**: Yes, he has. Often. Sometimes I question his sincerity, though. I want to believe him but feel so disconnected from him. My mom is so different. With my mom I feel very connected and truthfully loved. With my father it's just not the same.

***Sonya*:** Did you ask him his view of your relationship?
Homeless and Searching: He elaborated on his view of me as his daughter during his interview.
He has a distorted view of women altogether, I think. He said his mom acted like a promiscuous woman. He said he didn't want me to mimic her behavior as a loose lady. He didn't respect her. He didn't treat either of his wives the best so that only says to me he doesn't value women. I could be wrong. History tends to tell stories but the strength of God can overturn this. If he didn't' know how to love himself, I don't see now how he could have loved my mother or his children. I firmly believe the first relationship a man has with a women is with his mother so it's important he knows how to honor, protect, cherish, love and respect his mother. A good man does this, in my view.
***Sonya*:** Talk to me about generational curses.
Homeless and Searching: I think my father needs healing, of past or even present hurts. Because of his sins, I think we as his children have suffered greatly without even realizing why we may suffer at times. I strongly believe what the Bible says about the sins of the father in *Exodus 20:5-6*.
***Sonya*:** Did your father talk about God?
Homeless and Searching: Yes, after becoming a Christian. He did not speak of Jesus as we were children but now as we've become adults he does often. He declared himself a Jesus freak a long time ago, and as a result we've not been able to just have balanced conversation with him about real life. I use to limit

myself to ten minutes to deal with him over the phone, but this has improved since I've become more focused on my relationship with the Lord. Fathers, do you really think this is a good thing? I pose this question because you never know what your kids are thinking.

Sonya: So he's a hearer of the word but not a do-er.

Homeless and Searching: I have to go into a tunnel to communicate with him, meaning I shut down only to listen. I'm rarely speaking about me or any of my thoughts or needs anymore.

Sonya: A lot of people would ask, Is she crazy? He doesn't accept you, you never felt truly supported, and yet you still communicate with him. Did you choose to start back-talking to him?

Homeless and Searching: I'm torn because the Bible says we are to honor our father and mother. Since I love God and want to obey His Word I try, but my father makes this very hard sometimes with some of the things he still says that tend to stick to me. The difference is that the words don't hurt anymore. The difference now is that the things he says anger me since they come across as foolish and ignorant in nature and I no longer live in denial. He angers me and I respond truthfully. For him, my approach is not so great because it's more defensive in nature. I feel as if I'm fighting my abuser after lying dormant and taking blows for many years. Now I fight back!

Sonya: That's where the unconditional love comes from God.

Homeless and Searching: To protect me I now am selective about talking to him. This protection mechanism for me seems to work. I don't know any other way to do this without exposing myself to anger that I'd rather live without. I can no longer bear to hear bad information from him. Often times I tell him that I don't receive what he's saying if it hinders me in mind and spirit.

Sonya: So what are your terms?

Homeless and Searching: Listening, not speaking so quickly when talking with him, and a little dialogue here and there. When he starts to talk differently I distance myself before getting angry enough to hang up. Also surface conversation; I can only relate to him on the surface. I'm not capable of deep conversations with him any longer. I do more listening than anything. I am so disconnected and I don't think he realizes just how disconnected I am. The way we children communicate with him is different from the way we talk with my mother. I almost have to act like I'm flipping the script with him when he says something destructive to me.

Sonya: Do you want a relationship with him?

Homeless and Searching: I do, but I think about losing myself by having a relationship with him sometimes. I want to be able to communicate with him because he's my father. It's ideal to have a relationship because I realize Satan loves division within the family. To have to think about this very thing hurts, but I see him as a hurt person hurting people. I went to the country where he grew up and realized that he may not have learned to love or communicate because of his surrounding environment. This is no reason to speak to his children or wives the way he did or sometimes still does when allowed. He tore my mother down, physically, mentally, and verbally. With her children, he tore us down verbally.

***Sonya*:** How was the communication in his home?
Homeless and Searching: From what he shared, he didn't have that positive influence in his home and I can see how he wouldn't know how to create a peaceful environment in his own home. We have accepted him for who he is at this point in our lives. My prayer is that, within reason, we'll have a fruitful relationship going forward, because I believe God's Word and what it says. *Mark 11:23* says you will have what you say. I say that in time God will help develop a fruitful relationship among all of us, including with dad. Sometimes, I don't think he'll give up being in denial that he's not been there for us in the way we wanted and needed as his family. I do see growth, though, and tend to be open to God's will for the father-daughter relationship. I've surrendered in this area of my life and have grown comfortable in doing so. God knows my heart and desire concerning it all.

My mother says, "He is not capable of loving another human being." I've interpreted that statement for years to say, I've come to a place of acceptance but will never give up on my father. My Heavenly Father can heal us all and mend all brokenness.

Sonya: What's normal for us may not be normal for others. Maybe he's trying to make up for being a dad…Spiritually; you all aren't on the same level. Domestic violence dictates and when you are and aren't disciplined.

Homeless & Searching: He said something recently to insult my studies: "Going to school isn't going to make you a millionaire." Why start a war with someone who has war within them? It took a lot for me to get to this point of refraining from a major conservation. I have never called him "Dad." He disconnected us very early in life. A question for the dads out there: do you see yourself here? We were disconnected from the start.

Sonya: What does the number eight mean?

Homeless and Searching: He wasn't there for the first eight days of my life after being born. He left me at age eight, he wasn't there when I had my baby at the age twenty-eight and he fought my mom in public when I was eight. We had a big fall out in 2008. I thought the number eight meant new beginnings. I fully accept it for the way it is; the only difference now is I accept my father for who he is, realizing that, regardless of transgressions, he did the best he could with what he knew. I expect nothing. In God, though, I can expect the impossible (*Matthew 19:26*).

I think about his funeral and what we'll do as his children or what people will say. Am I just suppressing grief to come when he passes or am I truly okay with this disconnection? I had mixed emotions at times about telling this story but fathers need to know the impact they have on their children when the relationship is unhealthy.

Sonya: I don't think any child that has disconnected with a parent is okay with it, but maybe you've accepted it.

Homeless and Searching: No, you're right but disconnection has become a safe haven. My only sanity I have when communicating with him is to stay disconnected. Otherwise, I'm guilty of allowing myself to be exposed to the potential of being angered—since I've gone past the point of being hurt.

Sonya: I do know the Word is powerful and I haven't dealt with where you are. You could call those things that are not as though they were, as in Romans 4:17. I have to call it into existence. You have to speak those things because the Devil wants to destroy the family and the head of the family for that matter. The head is the father.

Homeless and Searching: What's sad is that I see how Satan has been victorious in that area in our family. I seem to believe most of his fathering years, my father reproduced as an unbeliever. Since he's now a believer I see where life has changed, so I know—both from what you say and from (*Matthew 19:26*)—that what you say is true.

Sonya: I commend you for trying because there are a lot of people who would not even try. So talk to me about looking for love from men in the wrong places. When did you first realize that?

Homeless and Searching*:* There are two points I need to make here: the rejection aspect with men and the rejection aspect with my father. I went on a vacation in 2008—that number eight again—and decided to take the time to get to know myself again by reading all of the journals that I'd written since I began journal writing in the third grade, at the age of eight. I immediately noticed a trend in all the journals I had been writing in, starting from third grade and continuing for twenty years after that. I'd considered this a show me-me session and realized that I've been searching for love from men for as long as I can remember. I never felt my heart had a home. I sense the reason for feeling homeless and searching was the situation at home and the fact that I never got to be daddy's little girl. The father is honored in the Spanish culture and he took that from us. For that, I have to admit I've often subjected myself to unhealthy relationships or relationships that compromise the true essence and gift that I am, just for the sake of having a man around. It's shameful, but the truth. Fathers, save your daughters from this ahead of time and love them at home so they'll make healthy choices outside the home.

So as a protection measure I often had a problem asking for what I deserve because of early rejection from my dad. The embarrassment and feeling so small always kept me unwilling to ask for what I needed. There are certain things in relationships I know I should have gotten but I didn't ask. That's not to say that men have never asked me for things. The Word says you have not because you ask not (*Matthew 7:7*). My father tore me down as a kid and made me feel so bad asking for anything, so I didn't then and wouldn't for years. I'd always associate my need with the anguish I felt when asking my dad for help. This usually prevented me from asking any man for anything so that rejection or shame would not be a part of the conversation. Hear me clearly, fathers, there's still more to fathering than just providing financially for your kids.

It wasn't until I was in a healthy relationship that I got comfortable asking a man for anything. Even so, it would still bring me anguish sometimes to do so. My father taught me through his damaging words that I should ask no one for anything since I associated this with rejection. However, I learned that the right man will want to aid my needs and be there for me and that it's okay to want the help of a man in your life. At the time my significant other helped with this a lot and helped me to get better with being open about what he could help with when needed. He was financially generous and, more importantly, showed me that it's okay to lean on another person. Praise God for that.

The realization of what state my self-esteem and self-perception was came from reading my diaries. I sought a lot of fatherly gestures in my previous relationships. Some men made me feel like they were a dad to me even though they were not dad or even a man I wanted to be with long-term. What I latched on to was that they may have been over-protective of me and it felt good since I never had that from my father. If it was a form of attention and if he was overly concerned all the time, I saw this as proper. Fathers, which would you prefer: for you to be the overseer and protector of your daughter, or Joe Shmo from wherever? I'm just asking.

***Sonya*:** Have you ever been abused by boyfriends?

Homeless and Searching: Yes, by two boyfriends.

***Sonya*:** So what is it about domestic violence that says you won't be in another relationship like that again?

Homeless and Searching: *John 10:10* says Jesus came so that we have life and have life more abundantly. Why did Jesus die if I'm going to live in mess and a lack of abundance? That is purely the answer: choose better to have better. More importantly, God loves me. God's validation tells me to no longer be in a violent relationship.

***Sonya*:** How do you protect yourself going forward or how do you know that you're not still looking for a father in relationships?

Homeless and Searching: I don't know that I'm not. Honestly, I feel as if the characteristics I want in my husband—protection, affirmation, love—are similar to that of a father. I don't see this as being wrong, though.

***Sonya*:** I think about that myself because my dad died when I was three-and-a-half from cancer and so I've never had a father figure. My uncles weren't positive figures either. This makes me wonder if I'll look for a

parental figure in my spouse. I think certain things should be parallel with a husband and father. Good point.
Homeless and Searching: I agree!
Sonya: Provide and protect are the two characteristics that should be parallel. What has helped you to develop your relationship with God?
Homeless and Searching: Through trials and tribulations and realizing that you can't get up from the ground without God's unchanging hand. I realized God is the ultimate source of all resources.
Sonya: What do you hope will come from this book?
Homeless and Searching: I hope that people will realize that it's not just their family that may struggle with these types of issues. There are many families that have to find a place of peace to live beyond destruction and despair.

Even though they may have been through all types of challenges, this book can serve as a testimony and reassure them that you can go on to seek healing for all involved. I had to come to a place of surrendering my feelings of inadequacy, despair, and insecurity for the lack of a loving relationship with my father for that loving, fulfilled relationship I desire with my Heavenly Father. His Word tells us we have life because of his son's death and actually that life should be lived in abundance (*John 10:10*).

The book serves men and women alike. It's definitely for that woman who did not have that flesh-and-blood father present in her life, or who had a father there who didn't provide emotional support. Reading the story of someone who has been in the same position can only make them realize the need to seek healing and be an eye-opener to those who seek healing.

When you don't get healing, you get hindrances. When you're not healed it tends to hold you back in other areas of your life where you need to be clear and free of emotional distractions. It's similar to buying a home with a bad title to it. You have to clear the title so the new owners can own the property free and clear. If you don't get healing you'll live within walls and boundaries that are self-imposed.

Sonya: Any resentment toward your dad?

Homeless and Searching: If I'm being honest, sure. I still see this as a work in progress but again I seek God's will opposed to my own. The funny thing is that this first relationship with a man didn't prove to be so great! Then I resented a lot of things. However, I've learned to forgive my father. "Father for they know not what they do," as Jesus said on the cross. I think my father has tried for a better relationship with his children in these past few years. Sometimes the more he pushes being the father we needed years ago now that we're adults; we seem to push in the opposite direction. I speak for myself on this but I sense, my siblings agree. We sometimes resent him trying to tell us what to do and often times withdraw or exclude him from our decision making. Fathers, this is all avoidable by being in the lives of your children all the way through, not

just occasionally. Sure, there are absent mothers, too, so for those fathers who are present, I salute you.
Sonya: Do you recall what you were thinking when he told ya'll not to call him dad?
Homeless and Searching: I remember thinking, "What kind of stuff is this?" I was laughing. "We can't call you dad?" I don't quite remember my age but I remember thinking to myself that this was crazy. My hope for the book is also that fathers, my own father included, will see the truth in what we're saying here. Reading this book may make it real for some but the intended purpose is for people to realize they are not alone and to seek healing for themselves and their families. Those hurting will need faith, along with perseverance and prayer. Through the anguish and abuse, that's what got us through it.

When first reading the interviews, I was so tempted to cry. My mother shared with me that she asked God to allow her to see her children become adults. She stated that on many days she was so miserable and her prayer was for God to help her leave him. In a sense, she felt as if she needed him to raise us but soon realized that if she didn't leave when and how she did, we'd all be crazy or worse. She made a calculated decision for the welfare of her children, and especially for her own welfare.
Sonya: Was this book therapeutic for you?
Homeless and Searching: I have mixed feelings. It has been hard because it's been sad—depressing in a sense—and sometimes a burden to write. I carried it for

years in my mind and heart. When I came to know Christ, then and only then could I be obedient and really go forward with publishing this experience. I realized that this experience isn't only for me but for all who've endured similar experiences. This book was written for such a time as this. God knew the perfect timing.

***Sonya*:** Since you're a mother, how do you want to see your daughter's relationship with her father different than your own relationship with your father?

Homeless and Searching: My hope is that she will have a fruitful relationship with her dad and that he doesn't relax in knowing she needs him daily. I sometimes see resemblances in how his daughter craves his attention like I did as a little girl. As a caring parent, I'd like to see her be her father's priority so my story isn't repeated. My priority is looking out for her and I pray that his eyes will be open enough to see her as a gift so that treasuring and making time with her are a priority. Therefore eliminating the idea of her resenting him later in life. History does have a tendency to repeat itself, so my desire isn't for her to hurt when she craves his undivided attention. Apparently excuses are easy for anyone & often timeless, like my own father. I know she's a priority for me but sometimes the daughter is only affirmed by the father. This I know from personal experience. In her case she's learning about the Heavenly Father at a very early age, so she'll understand the beauty and gift of God's love when her birth father isn't available. For her, this is a gift early in life.

Sonya: So maybe when you meet men you should ask questions like, What is your relationship with your own father?

Homeless and Searching: I'd ask, but *seeing* the relationship with the father is even better. Also, the mother. I'd tell women to definitely ask this question because it's something you need to know. That's going to be a picture of what you could experience in the event you marry and have children with that person.

We went through so much in my immediate family. My mother took my younger siblings and me to counseling to try and work out our issues when we were minors, but it didn't help. I guess she felt this would assist us in working through our issues. Back then I can remember being in such turmoil and denial on the inside because of what was taking place within my family. I would never talk or open up with the counselor. I remember feeling ashamed and embarrassed about my true feelings. Now I realize family counseling goes a long way and could actually help those who are willing. Sadly, we know in our community some families don't see the need to get counseling.

As a result of all of the distress, one of my brothers wrote backwards in school and my mom broke out in hives. The apparent result of all the wear and tear from being in an unhealthy marriage filled us with problems. From there we had to put our lives together in a single parent household, one day at a time.

Sonya: What do you think your family's response will be to the book?

Homeless and Searching: They were all sincere and honest when speaking during our talks. They both opened up and didn't spare any feelings; no one held back what they felt. I think they'll all be surprised at what the other carried inside of their heart.

Sonya: Do you think the book was therapeutic for your family members?

Homeless and Searching: I think my mom can appear bitter or even angry at times when we talk about my father. I remember anger in her voice when she spoke about him, but who can blame her? I tended to notice how her voice would rise when it came to discussing my father. Again, I can't blame her but only hope deliverance is near if it hasn't already taken place in some form or fashion. I remember her stating that she forgives him. She hasn't forgotten, though. I don't think she ever will. Again, I can't blame her either. I don't expect or suggest she forgive, forget, or let it go, because she endured all with him. I pray daily for her and will continue to do so.

Sonya: Hopefully this will give a new beginning to you and your father. It will be God's doing and will. My prayer is for us all to be connected to our fathers, both our birth fathers and our Heavenly Father.

Homeless and Searching: I leave it up to God from here on out. My ability is to pray for deliverance for myself and for everyone involved so family relationships can be restored for us and all families around the world. Here's our home after the divorce.

On those very bricks at Heatherly Drive, Uncovered, Silent Rage, Rejected, and Searching—learned the following:

229 Heatherly Drive

- The Greenville police department had no problem profiling little black children.
- Different neighborhood rivalries were a fact of life.
- Who you could and who you could not trust in the neighborhood, from conversations with other children who'd been terrorized.
- All girls aren't nice.

- All boys aren't nice (one neighbor tried his best to take sexual advantage of me when I was a little girl).
- My big brother would beat up anyone in the neighborhood for trying to touch me as a little girl.
- A jealous bully lived nearby.

Watching the mail box at Heatherly Drive taught me about lies, and how our father so rarely supported us financially. He'd say he had sent the child support money, but disappointment after disappointment made life unbearable sometimes. He did occasionally send the bare minimum ($60.00 per week), but not even for all the children he'd fathered. So in actuality we received $20.00 per child per week. No wonder my mom always struggled.

Fathers, you can see how if you aren't the biggest voice in your children's ear, then someone, some place, or some entity will be the biggest voice in their ear, and sometimes these voices aren't for the good. Parents have been called to be gatekeepers and, since I'm a daughter, I honestly believe the loudest voice in a daughter's ear should be her father's. Will you be yours? I can't tell you what to do, but can tell you from experience what will happen if you do nothing.

I wonder how teenagers go through different stages of teen pregnancy and sexual issues without proper guidance. Could it be that we aren't teaching them in the first institution of learning, which is the family? Statistics on teen pregnancy support our belief that we probably aren't shedding enough light on the matter in our own homes. Given our personal experiences, this could very well be the reason that a lot of young people find themselves in compromised positions.

I pledge to fully educate those under me on sex, disease, abortion, birth control, ovulation and menstrual cycles, babies, sexual temptation and the like. We have to educate our children. As a role model to the younger generation, I feel obligated to teach kids about Christ and his sacrifice for our lives and how to live holy. Further explaining that our body is a temple and that it isn't to be treated without thought by having premature sex is a priority for me. Trust me: I've learned drastically from not following the Word on what it says about premarital sex, sin that is.

I'd tell any young person that they should abstain from having sex until marriage. When a parent does not, lives are molded in different ways, and not always in a good way. I don't speak from a theoretical point of view here, but from personal experience and practicality.

Fathers, some things are important for you to teach your kids so that certain things you experienced in your childhood that you don't want repeated will not come to pass. Pray, pray, and pray some more that the karma and generational curses in your family tree don't repeat themselves.

Fathers, do you ever wonder why you're grown children may not be involved in your life or in touch with you as you expect? Spend some time reflecting on just what type of love you gave them when they were younger or perhaps the type of involvement you had with them as growing people. Self-evaluation is always good to do so you can recognize reasons and move forward, correct these things if still possible.

Developing as a child without loving support from your father tends to leave you feeling "Uncovered," and as a result he had to learn to fend for yourselves. Even though we all needed support, our father was never there for us. How many of you who come from divided households can sense similarities with what we're sharing with you? Fathers have a profound effect. Mothers do, too, but since there are so many single mother households, this book is a reflection of what the absence of the father can do to a household. It's great when the mother acknowledges the Heavenly Father as the head of household in such circumstances.

You see, I may have suppressed some things from memory by choice but each one of us have been affected differently. Each of us has held different things in our hearts. In other words, our memories have been vivid enough to remember different events that happened in our home that affected all of us.

I have over the years reflected back to that payphone in Judson at Easley Bridge Road by the church. That was where I, oftentimes, was the one as the delegated communicator who called our father to inquire about the child support. That was also the phone where on many occasions I was made to feel worse than before I called because of the verbal abuse. I remember being told not to call and ask for money. I remember being told many things other than, "Yes, I'll send money for my three children to eat."

What I later learned is that my father would back up verbal abuse with scripture after he left the Islamic faith and became a Christian. On rare occasions I would hang the phone feeling a little affirmed but many times I was left in confusion. I had made a phone call to gain the security of a father's love and had been disappointed again.

However, as I repeat this thought, I've come to a place where I trust God for the type of daughter-father relationship that will exist between me and my father from now on. With the closeness of the Heavenly Father, I've since become secure and reaffirmed and have come to discern right from wrong and yes from no. I've shed the feeling of insecurity about anything that I did before. I've gained trust, love, support, wisdom, and everything a daughter could hope for in God who is the loving Father I've needed for so many days. Over the years my siblings and I ponder our memories of Greyhound and the twenty-six-hour bus rides from the East coast to Texas every summer didn't offer much laughter. We had to pack lunches and lay on our own pillows to avoid lying on seats that were sat in by lots of people, not realizing that a lot of those people we accompanied on the bus to go visit dad were child rapists, murderers, and the like. Even then, although we didn't know it, the grace of God carried us through from Greenville to Dallas. We were riding across the country on a bus full of strangers without adult supervision, without cell phones, having to change buses in the middle of the night, remembering to transfer in old bus stations in odd towns and pray it all worked out in the absence of both our parents. It's sad because we clearly realized once in the West that dad could have elected to put us on an airplane and fly us instead. Flying us would have been safer and much quicker than being on a Trailways or Greyhound bus for a day or more. This was simply crazy.

· And since I was the eldest sibling, it was fully my responsibility to arrange our travel on the road, pay attention to switching buses, even if at 3 a.m. There's no way I can envision such a thing for children now days. The option to bus us instead of fly us was simply a lack of priority on his behalf, since our mother paid 98% of our living expenses, carrying much of the load throughout the year.

What grace God extended to all of us children on all of those traveling experiences! We could have been raped, molested, kidnapped, or even murdered, never to be seen again, all to see a father who could afford to fly us. We were too young to realize it then but we certainly know the truth now. To know better is to do better.

Fathers, when you don't financially support your children, their mothers contribute to the statistics of being in the highest poverty bracket: single mothers with children. A lot of African-American single mother households contribute to these stats. Do you ever take a head count of how many black, single mothers are at the park on Sunday with their little ones, as opposed to how many families of other races are picnicking at the park? I'm just asking, dads. Fathers, let's do better. I'm asking and pleading with you for better relationships with your children. Fathers, you matter, this matters, your daughters matter.

Taking the chance to pull out of the parking lot of BI-LO on Mauldin Road near Highway 385 to ride a bus mid cross country and to arrive safe and sound was simply the grace of God. I can remember our first Trailways ride and seeing the image of a disappearing mother as we left the bus terminal on our 1st trip. What in the world gave her the comfort or strength to realize her three youngest children would be okay for the next few days without a cell phone or a way to check on us? I know: our Heavenly Father. Praise God, though surely she was still worried beyond belief until she received confirmation that we arrived safely. She probably got little sleep and secretly cried to herself in fear. Looking back, just the thought of it makes me cry. Thank God, for His magnificent grace. He is amazing, awesome, and worthy to be praised. He is Jehovah Jirah, Jehovah Nese.

Fathers, we need you not as the competitor but the leader. Please be our father. By now I know you think I'm making this up. I assure you that I'm not. I only want to expose the truth, not harm anyone any more than they already have been. I know my dad was and still could be hurting, hence the reason he continuously talks about my mother to this day.

Fathers, take the time to instill confidence in your children and educate them on how to approach the opposite gender when they reach an age appropriate for dating. This is ideal. It will boost their confidence knowing that approaching women is natural; for young ladies, it will be healthy to know that a man approaching them with respect is also appropriate. The Bible is clear in stating that "He, who finds a wife, finds favor from the Lord" (*Proverbs 18:22*). Without taking the time with your sons to enlighten them on your experiences with women—especially those positive relationships with your mothers, wife, sisters, etc.—they are prone to fall and make many mistakes on their own.

As of this writing, as the only girl in the household, I'm compelled to pray more for my brothers. I pray this works. From the confusion we all have not fully recovered from the pain but know that God can do the impossible, in addition I know that healing, forgiveness and living whole is also possible in God. Some of us have consulted the love of our Heavenly Father but not all of us. To date, I'd say my siblings as have operated in a spectrum of one that is "*rejected, uncovered,* in *silent rage,* and *withdrawn.*"

Chapter 7
"I Apologize"
—Me

I could say I'm sorry, but I won't. Instead I'll say, "I apologize." Saying I'm sorry, according to Webster's Dictionary, would mean that I feel regret, compunction, sympathy, and pity. It's not that I feel pity, sympathy, or even regret. In this case I want to apologize because Webster's Dictionary states an apology is an expression of one's regret for having been injured, insulted, or even wronged by another. To each of you reading this book, so that you will know well in advance that someone cares enough to apologize, I offer the following apologies.

Why do I take the liberty to do so? Mainly because, if you've not been formally apologized to by your mother or father, that apology might be necessary for closure. Your healing could be dependent on that very acknowledgement and apology.

I apologize for your father not being at your birth; not being there to see your first steps; not being there for your first words, which were probably "da-da"; not being there for the first birthday; not being there for your first day of pre-school, your first day of grade school, your first day of middle school; for not being there to see the many accolades you've achieved; for not being there when you had your first boyfriend or girlfriend; for not being there for prom, for high school graduation, for a college tour and selection of college, for your first day of college, for engagement, for your engagement party, for your wedding day, for the funeral of the other parent; for not being there when you gave birth to your children; for not being there for the purchase of your first home; for not being there to celebrate your many successes; for not being there for your first big job or your first promotion, and many that followed; for not being there to see your children grow up.

      There are so many things mothers and fathers need to be present for. I apologize for whoever was not there. I apologize. Trust me in many of these circumstances, I wish my flesh-and-blood father had been there, but know that our Heavenly Father has always been there and always will be. God bless you.

Chapter 8
Homeless to Found with the Heavenly Father

"I will be a Father to you, and you will be my sons and daughters, says the Lord Almighty."
—*2 Corinthians 6:18*

What my God can do! God is the Father of all. When you don't have a father as a result of abandonment, divorce, separation, or even perhaps death, you can always count on your Heavenly Father. You may have not grown up with that loving daddy but the Heavenly Father has always been there. He was there then and He's here now. Have you accepted a relationship with God the Father and his son Jesus? He has been the Father to me, the daddy to me, on many days when my flesh-and-blood father was unavailable physically, mentally, or perhaps verbally.

Psalms 65:8 says that God is "a father to the fatherless, a defender of widows, is God in his holy dwelling." *Proverbs 23:22* says, "Listen to your father who gave you life." See, fortunately for some, they realize early on that God the Father is what we need. He is there to console us when we experience that first heartbreak from the opposite gender; he's there to steer you in all circumstances and situations. While you may not always consult him for simple things that we deal with daily, he's always there to lead his sheep. God is the shepherd that tends to the sheep. You can rest in knowing that he will not steer you wrong. Have you ever felt as if you have no male protecting you if you're a woman? Has your birth father passed on? I can only imagine a bride who is waiting in the church for an absent father to walk her down the aisle. I'd imagine her truly missing that father who she always pictured escorting her into marriage, her biggest commitment in life. This is sad for those who don't know God as the Father. You don't have to ever feel as if your father isn't there. This is simply a choice that you make. Consult God on all matters, not just those that you cannot figure out.

Chapter 9
Seen Through These Eyes

"But from everlasting to everlasting the Lord's love is with those who fear him and his righteousness with their children's children".
—*Psalms 103:17*

You should know this was not easy to do. The words have been formed for many years but were never put to ink until one day when enough was simply enough. Still, writing this exposed the hurt that had nowhere to hide any longer; the unexpressed anger that ran for cover could no longer be hid; the frustration that stood in line with bitterness, pain, resentment, and just plain anger all had to come out from their hibernation. As a result of struggling to put this book together for others, you have read the heart of a daughter. Thankfully, in writing this, I discovered that my relationship with the Heavenly Father was the one to prevail, the one to heal, the one to help, the one to mend, and the one to provide hope to all. My prayer is simple: that you'd be healed, that you'd be awakened, but more importantly that you'd forgive. Yes, we have to forgive. Forgive those who hurt you.

This is a gift, a gift to the fatherless: those who felt they grew up without their father, those who grew up fatherless even if he was there in the household, those children who never knew that the Father has been there all the time. My question to you is this: since you felt fatherless, have you discovered your real Father?

This book is also an aid to fathers who want to truly understand the impact they have on their families, the impact they have on those who are entrusted to their care, particularly their children. Hopefully you now understand the full impact of your absence or even your presence. My hope was that this book reveals just how much a daughter has seen and been impacted by both her birth father and God, her Heavenly Father. Thank you for taking the time to sow into your life and the life of those around you by adding a well-intended aid to your life and the lives of those who need you—and if you're a parent, more than anything the ones who need you are your children.

Chapter 10
A Daughter's Prayer
A prayer to the Father for us…..
—Me

Father, I pray in Jesus' name that you would release every family member—mother, father, and child—from any hindering spirits that may linger from past hurts, hindrances, wrongdoings, and abuse in any form or fashion, known and unknown, so that life can be abundantly greater going forward.

I also pray that those reading this book may see the need to want new life with their fathers, mothers, siblings, and anyone in the family that they feel has wronged, abused, harmed, or hindered them so that they will be free from this day forth.

Father, I also apologize for those and to those for their journey if they have never been apologized to from the one who has hurt them. I pray for the one who has never apologized to those they've harmed even if they are too ashamed, embarrassed, or proud to do so themselves.

I ask for your healing hands to touch every person reading this, release them from hurt, anger, bitterness, and anything that will keep them from truthfully loving themselves, you, or anyone else in their lives worthy to be loved.

Father, keep them in the palms of your hands, comfort them where and when they need to be comforted. Send the right people to them, and dismiss those that shouldn't be with them any longer, so that they may seek you diligently for new life through salvation.

In Jesus name I pray, your daughter Felicia. Amen.

Meet the Author

Felicia holds a Bachelor's of Science degree in Psychology and Christian Counseling from Liberty University and currently studying to become a Licensed Marriage and Family Therapist.

Smith is the Host and Producer of the television talk show Relate-2-Clinic. In addition, Smith facilitates the ***Father Factor Workshop***, designed to strengthen the bonds between fathers and their families.

As a writer, speaker, and professional, Felicia's mission is to work to educate the public about the dangers of fatherless households, and to promote the health of American families.

Please contact Queen Dream Publishing if you would like additional copies of this book and for the Author's speaking availability at your upcoming event.

Email: info@queendreamz.com

www.queendreamz.com

www.ingramcontent.com/pod-product-compliance
Lightning Source LLC
Chambersburg PA
CBHW020900090426
42736CB00008B/450